STRANGE

THE YEAR IN WEIRDNESS

DAYS #2

BY THE EDITORS OF
FORTEAN TIMES

CADER BOOKS

ANDREWS AND MCMEEL
A UNIVERSAL PRESS SYNDICATE COMPANY
KANSAS CITY

Thank you for buying this Cader Book—we hope you enjoy it. And thanks as well to the store that sold you this, and the hardworking sales rep who sold it to them. It takes a lot of people to make a book (even a strange one). Here are some of the many who were instrumental:

EDITORIAL:
Rufus Griscom, Steve Baumgartner, Jackie Kramer, Jake Morrissey, Nora Donaghy, Polly Blair

DESIGN:
Charles Kreloff

COPY EDITING/PROOFING:
Roland Ottewell, Bill Bryan

PRODUCTION:
Carol Coe, Cathy Kirkland

LEGAL:
Renee Schwartz, Esq.

FORTEAN CONSULTANTS:
Mike Dash, Bob Rickard, Joe McNally

And thanks to Bill Barker for permission to use the Schwa symbol. For more information write Box 6064, Reno, NV 89513 or visit:
http://www.theschwacorporation.com

Copyright © 1997
Fortean Times and Cader Company Inc.
All rights reserved. No part of this book may be used or reproduced in any manner whatsoever without written permission of the Publisher. Printed in the United States of America.

Library of Congress
Cataloging-in-Publication Data
Strange days #2 : the year in wierdness
    / by the editors of Fortean
Times. — 1st ed.
        p.   cm.
    Includes bibliographical references.
    ISBN 0-8362-2767-0 (pb)
    1. Curiosities and wonders.
        2. Parapsychology.
        I. Fortean times.
AG243.S836 1997
031.02—dc21   97-6688
                                      CIP

ISBN: 0-8362-2767-0

April 1997

First edition
10 9 8 7 6 5 4 3 2 1

If you would like to share any thoughts about this book, or are interested in other books by us, please write to:

Cader Books
38 E. 29 Street
New York, NY 10016

Or visit our cool new web site:
http://www.caderbooks.com

ATTENTION:
SCHOOLS AND BUSINESSES
Andrews and McMeel books are available at quantity discounts with bulk purchase for educational, business, or sales promotional use. For information, please write to: Special Sales Department, Andrews and McMeel, 4520 Main Street, Kansas City, Missouri 64111.

CONTENTS

....

THE HUMAN WORLD
....

BREAD HEAD, THE BREAST MILK VIGILANTE,
AND OTHER ODDITIES...

V

THE ANIMAL WORLD

MANICURED CROCS, THE CHUPACABRAS, AND OTHER ODDITIES...

THE NATURAL WORLD

PULSARS, EROTIC CHEWING GUM, AND OTHER ODDITIES…

THE PARANORMAL WORLD

SPARKLING SHIRTS, CITIES ON THE MOON, AND OTHER ODDITIES...

WEIRD STUFF HAPPENS

What can I say about a year in which a man in Uniondale, New York, held 140 chickens hostage; fossil remains of the ninth type of Australopithecus were found in Indonesia; crocodiles wandered on the freeways of California and the British Midlands; and a Japanese porn star was crucified in the Philippines . . . except Yippee! For us at *Fortean Times* it meant business as usual. It was a great year for what we call Forteana, miscellaneous notes and observations of anomalies and discoveries from all over the world, gleaned from the far side of whatever passes for reality.

Unusually, we didn't hear of as many falls of fish as in previous years—only one occurrence springs to mind—and there was a decrease in sightings of large predatory cats in Britain, which seem to have peaked over the previous two years. Instead, we had a marvellous run of panics and flaps.

Beginning in September 1995 (too late for inclusion in *Strange Days #1*) there was a frenzy of interest as statues of Hindu gods appeared to be drinking up milk offered to them on spoons. Word spread via the Internet and the phenomenon was soon flourishing in temples in India, Malaysia, and other Hindu communities worldwide. As reports trailed off, there was a run, into 1996, of weeping Madonnas in Italy—in particular, a statue in Civitavechia, which shed tears of "male, human blood," drew crowds at the rate of 5,000 a week. Towards the close of the year, at a time of rising tension between the Jewish and Palestinian communities, an icon of Jesus in Bethlehem's Basilica of the Nativity was observed weeping bloody tears. In August 1996 came the stunning news that a meteorite found in the Antarctic came from Mars and contained tiny microfossilized structures which, if they occurred on Earth, would be associated with bacterial life. Although the announcement by NASA exobiologists was later qualified by the caution of their scientific colleagues, it may yet prove to be one of the most significant discoveries in the history of man for, if it pans out, it will be the first unequivocal evidence that we are not alone in this vast universe. Either life was kick-started on Earth by organic material arriving from elsewhere on meteorites or life can indeed spring up easily anywhere where the conditions are just right—the so-called Goldilocks prescription.

Of course the extraterrestrial life that most folks have in mind is not some lowly bacterial slime but the kind Mulder and Scully hunt down in *The X-Files*. 1996 was the year interest in this program went ballistic, followed by *Independence Day* and a slew of TV spin-offs and lookalikes. Most of these celebrated another popular ingredient, the belief that the government (or a secret group within government) knows that aliens exist and may even be in collusion with them. The September issue of Penthouse boldly claimed to take the wraps off some honest-to-God photos of a dead alien, but diligent researchers soon discovered that the magazine had paid thousands of dollars for snapshots taken by a tourist of

WHAT'S "FORTEAN"?

Charles Hoy Fort (1874–1932)

Fortean Times: The Journal of Strange Phenomena, from which much of this book is taken, is a monthly magazine of news, reviews and research on extraordinary experiences, observations, behavior, creatures and beliefs. It was founded in 1973 to continue the work of Charles Fort. Throughout his life, Fort was skeptical about scientific explanations, observing how scientists argued according to their own beliefs and that inconvenient data was ignored, suppressed, discredited or explained away (which is quite a different thing from explaining something).

Fort, born in Albany, New York, spent most of his life in the New York Library and the British Museum Library amassing a vast database of notes which found their way into *The Book of the Damned* (1919), *New Lands* (1923), *Lo!* (1931) and *Wild Talents* (1932).

His dictum "One measures a circle beginning anywhere" expresses his philosophy of Continuity in which everything is in an intermediate state between extremes. Fort also supported the idea of universe-as-organism and the transient nature of all apparent phenomena.

Today, Fortean Times gathers similar materials using the Internet, computers and a growing network of readers who participate by submitting news clippings.

an alien dummy in the International UFO Museum at Roswell. No doubt some people believe that was part of a conspiracy, one way or another.

The propensity of the public to panic over aliens was exemplified by the *Chupacabras* scare, in which a blood-sucking alien creature was blamed for the deaths of great numbers of livestock around the Gulf of Mexico. First appearing on Puerto Rico, the panic spread to Hispanic communities on the American continent before it died down. Almost side-by-side with the Goatsucker saga, a story emerged from Brazil that

promises to rival the crashed UFO at Roswell as it grows in complexity. I refer to the claims that five aliens were flushed out of hiding near the town of Varginha, in the state of Minas Gerais, and were last seen by many witnesses being spirited away by the army. It is, of course, officially denied.

Elsewhere in the world, alien anxiety rode equally high. In India, a rash of deaths and disappearances of children was blamed on a "pig-faced monster" with the power to lull people as it sneaks up, stealing babies from mothers' laps. Rationalists blamed the abductions on a crafty pack of wolves but, even after several wolves were killed, the incidents continued and the legendary pack was never found. Pious Navajos began making pilgrimages to a hogan at Rocky Ridge, near Big Mountain in Arizona, in the belief that two of the tribal deities had visited an old woman and her daughter, asking for a return to the "old ways." In the island country of Zanzibar, men quaked in their beds, fearing a visit from the *popobawa,* a terrible one-eyed dwarf with bat-wings and talons and a reputation for raping men as they slept. In California, remote-viewer Courtney Brown told the listeners to Art Bell's syndicated radio show that the comet Hale-Bopp had a mystery planet-sized companion—dubbed, by Art Bell himself, Hale-Mary—populated by reptilian creatures coming to save us from ourselves.

While that may have cheered up some people, for me the "feel good" story of the year owes nothing to muddled humans or beneficent aliens but everything to the mothering instinct of its heroine. In August, Binti Jua, an eight-year-old Western Lowland gorilla rescued a three-year-old boy who fell into the gorilla enclosure at Chicago's Brookfield Zoo. With her own baby on her back, she cradled the boy in her arms, fending off other gorillas as she placed the boy near a door where zookeepers could retrieve him.

As I look back on 1996, with its painful toll of lives from the conflicts in Bosnia, Rwanda, Chechnya and elsewhere, it is this display of humanity by an animal that I shall remember most. That and the fact that, after all the years of war and destructive bombing, the jungles of Indochina have yielded at least eleven species of animals previously unknown to zoologists with the possibility that there are other wonders awaiting discovery. Somehow it seems symbolic of both the unexpected and the way the familiar is often turned upside down . . . but that's also what I mean by "business as usual."

The stories presented in this volume were published in the *Fortean Times* during 1996—generally referred to in the text as "this year"—although you are bound to find some accounts of 1995 weirdness and occasional references to earlier events. All dates that do not include a year refer to 1996. As we believe, in noting our sources whenever possible, you will find an abbreviated list of references at the back of the book.

This volume uses the categories of our famed Strangeness Index (which begins on page XIV) as its organizing principle. In the best scientific tradition, data which did not fit into the available categories were generally ignored or shoehorned into one anyway. Much of the boxed material throughout the book reflects new trends in abnormal phenomena which became evident in the course of sifting through a year's worth of Fortean clippings. And at long last, the second annual "Schwascar" awards named for the omnipresent alien graphic created by Bill Barker in 1992, has come to signify the enigmatic or abnormal. These awards are presented for exceptionally weird occurrences.

BOB RICKARD
FOUNDER AND EDITOR
FORTEAN TIMES
JANUARY 1997

1997 STRANGENESS INDEX

The *Fortean Times'* expertly trained crew has been adding up the column inches again, to bring you our legendary barometer of the bizarre, the annual Strangeness Index. Sadly, we cannot accurately measure weirdness itself (yet); however, we are in an excellent position to measure how weird the world is *reported* to be, simply by examining the stories that have been sent to, and have appeared in, *Fortean Times*.

In order to quantify worldwide weirdness as accurately as possibly, we have broken down abnormal phenomena into the 34 representative categories below. Every year we compare the number of bizarre incidents reported in each category to the previous year. Increases are designated by up arrows, decreases by down arrows, and no change by horizontal arrows.

Though we generally rely upon our own archives of newspaper clippings and research in assessing weirdness levels, a spectacular increase in outside reporting on a topic which wasn't included in *Fortean Times* was still counted as an increase.

And speaking of increases . . . The discovery of traces of life in Martian meteorites, the success of *The X-Files, Independence Day* and their multitude of imitators, and the unprecedented interest in the Puerto Rican Goatsucker all contributed to a higher level of media interest in the weird, the wonderful and the uncanny in 1996 than we have seen in some time.

WORLDWIDE WEIRDNESS
FLUCTUATIONS IN 1996

THE HUMAN WORLD

STRANGE BEHAVIOR ↗
CULTS & CONSPIRACIES ↗
DEATHS & SUICIDES ↘
GENIUS & DISCOVERY ↘
HOAXES & PANICS →
INEPTITUDE & STUPIDITY ↗
ANTIQUITIES ↗

THE ANIMAL WORLD

OUT-OF-PLACE ANIMALS ↗
ATTACKS BY ANIMALS →
ATTACKS ON ANIMALS ↗
SWARMINGS ↘
NEW SPECIES FOUND ↗
MASS DEATHS →
MANIMALS ↗
WATER MONSTERS ↗

THE NATURAL WORLD

DISASTERS, NATURAL
& MAN-MADE ↗
BIOLOGICAL & MEDICAL ↗
EPIDEMICS & ILLNESS ↘
FALLS FROM THE SKY ↗
FIRES & SPONTANEOUS HUMAN
COMBUSTION →
METEOROLOGICAL
SUPERLATIVES ↗

GEOPHYSICAL ACTIVITY ↗
CROP CIRCLES ↘

THE PARANORMAL
WORLD

PSYCHICAL PHENOMENA →
PROPHECIES ↗
APPARITIONS ↘
IMAGES ↗
BAD LUCK →
GOOD LUCK ↗
MIRACLES ↘
POLTERGEISTS →
UFOS ↗
CLOSE ENCOUNTERS
& ALIEN ABDUCTIONS ↘
PARANORMAL EXPERIENCES →

Taking into account the ups and downs noted above, we have calculated that the world was 2.4% weirder last year than the year before.

How did we arrive at this?

When the original Index was created in 1992 each category was assigned a baseline value of 100. Starting with a total baseline value of 3,400 in 1992, the Index rose to 3,520 in 1993, fell to 3,450 in 1994, slipped back to its original value of 3,400 in 1995, and has now climbed to 3,480.

THE
HUMAN
WORLD

THE HUMAN WORLD

A German man found hoarding 422 sets of stolen false teeth, the technology to store a lifetime of memories on a single computer chip, and the loser of a bible-quoting contest murdering the victor by shooting him in the face (so much for the other cheek)—any news of bizarre, eery, or outrageously foolish human behavior rears its head in this section.

Last year provided, yet again, a bumper crop of human weirdness and wonder. Antiquities were well up, with a highlight being the discovery of a very early French settlement in South Carolina called Charles Fort. As ever, Strange Behavior—odd crimes, mysterious compulsions and downright high weirdness—is on the up. Stupidity remains second only to hydrogen in its ubiquity. Depressingly, Genius and Discovery are down again. Conspiracies got a massive boost from the dozens of theories about the mysterious crash of TWA Flight 800.

STRANGE BEHAVIOR

WALK THE TUBE

Police are puzzled by an apparent trend among early-risers in Christchurch, New Zealand, for walking a home appliance instead of a dog. On May 7, a man walking his dog in the Parklands saw two fellow early-risers trying to "walk" a wall oven. Two days later, a woman answered loud knocking at her door at 5:15 a.m. to be confronted by a man holding a color television set. He said he was having difficulty finding his way out of her property and appealed for help. She obliged and then checked that the television set was not hers.

Ten minutes later, police, called to an unrelated matter on a neighboring property, found the man still clutching the television set. Inquiries revealed the TV belonged to the man, but he could not explain why he was wandering around in the dark with it. "It has left us wondering if there are not enough dogs to go around," said Senior Sergeant Kortegast.

PECULIAR PRESS

MAN ORDERED TO MARRY COW
Monitor (Uganda),
October 2–4, 1995

BEIJING AWAITS "TOPLESS LESBIANS"
Irish Times, August 31, 1995

BULGE IN TROUSERS WAS ECSTASY
Luton on Sunday, September 13, 1995

SNUFF STIFF

People coming to see the film *Deadly Virus* in a Berlin cinema stepped over a dead usher's body in the darkened entrance, thinking he was a wax dummy promoting the film. Some of the moviegoers were even seen kicking him and walking on his back. Max Bauer had, in fact, suffered a fatal heart attack just before the film opened.

HELLO DEER

Police investigating an "obnoxious odor" coming from Michael Husar's apartment in Bethel Park, a suburb of Pittsburgh, Pennsylvania, found a headless deer carcass up to five days old. Husar, 32, said he found the dead doe, took it home, and had sex with it. He also drank some of its blood. The deer had been killed illegally with a crossbow.

TALKING PENIS AXED

An AIDS awareness campaign TV advertisement in Brazil featuring a talking penis called Braulio was axed by the government after men named Braulio complained that they were being ridiculed.

MONUMENTS OF INVENTION

A monument to rock star Frank Zappa has been erected in Vilnius, Lithuania, although the two had no connections. Vilnius officials felt sure

CREEPY CLOWNS

❧ In April 1994 a man in clown make-up robbed a bus in Guatemala. The nation was already gripped by panic over North American tourists allegedly kidnapping children to provide organs for transplants; the two topics melded into a fear of child-seizing "bandit clowns."

❧ A frenzy spread in Honduras as well. Parents and neighbors in San Pedro Sula had already caught one suspected clown-kidnapper, but fear peaked around Halloween 1995. A Mexican dressed as a clown was arrested for attempted abduction; police claimed ten missing children had been seized by van-driving bandit clowns during October's final week. On November 2 in a Tegucigalpa park, 60 clowns gathered to burn their costumes in protest.

❧ Closer to home, rumors of clown-kidnappers in vans gripped southeast Washington and Alexandria, Virginia, in June 1994, with nearly 100 reports. The first incident took place on the night of June 3 in Washington's Congress Heights neighborhood. An adolescent girl said that a man in his twenties, dressed in a red wig and nose, tried to lure her into a white '93 Ford van with Maryland plates by offering her candy. The police regarded most of the subsequent sightings as bogus, but by June 13, the firms of Fonzie the Clown and Balloons Inc. had received 15 cancellations from parents who didn't want clowns at their children's parties.

❧ In Capital Heights, Maryland, on June 7, 1994, two men dressed in bushy wigs and red clown noses climbed into the car of a 54-year-old woman at a traffic intersection. They pulled guns and forced her to drive to a local Pepsi bottling plant, where they blindfolded her and placed her in the trunk. She was driven elsewhere, led into a room and cut in the shoulder and the stomach before being released.

❧ On October 4, 1995, a man dressed in a red nose, wig and fake Dracula teeth convinced nurses at St. Andrew's Hospital in Billericay, England, that he was delivering a get-well telegram to a male patient. He found the patient, produced a sawed-off shotgun from a large bunch of flowers and shot him.

that he would have visited Lithuania, had he not died two years ago.

ALL YOU CAN EAT

Turkish police were hunting a woman who raids flower shops in Ankara and flees after eating the heads off roses. A few weeks later, a man in Thailand was submitted to psychiatric tests after breaking in to a

model's home in Bangkok and eating nine silk dresses.

SANITY CLAUSE

David Lynn Justice, 21, was jailed for 30 years last June for abducting two women at gunpoint outside a Houston restaurant in December 1993, making them buy Twinkies and caffeine pills, then forcing them on a

DENTAL DECOR

❧ To aid his fight against tooth decay, Dr. Yu, left, of China's Quingan County has built an elaborate eight-foot, two-inch-high pagoda of 28,000 rotting teeth. Each of the sections is made from the appropriate type of tooth: the giant molar at the bottom is made entirely of molars, rising up through bicuspids, with incisors at its crown. Best of all it glows in the dark thanks to the lights built into the sculpture's core.

❧ Police found a Hamburg, Germany apartment decorated with 422 sets of false teeth stolen by Daniel Slinger in ten years of thefts from dentists.

---

tour of Christmas lights. "He was depressed and wanted some company."

VEILED THREAT

The Kenyan government is to allow Muslim women to wear their veils in photographs for new national identity cards after they threatened a boycott if obliged to be portrayed without them.

I'M GONNA GET YOU SUCKLER

Police in Eureka, California, are hunting a woman who has been grabbing babies from total strangers and breastfeeding them. "Every child needs lactate nourishment," she told a shocked mother during the latest incident.

ROCKY REMEDY

A family of seven believe they have discovered an elixir of life. They are putting their faith in a potion made from rock dust. The idea came to ecologists Moira and Cameron Thomson of Auchterhouse, Australia, when trees damaged by acid rain recovered after wind blew a fine rock dust over them.

IN THE NAME OF GOD

On February 13, God was sent down for nine months in San Rafael, California, when he was found guilty of indecently exposing himself to a woman in a coffee shop. God, 68, has been arrested 18 times for similar offenses since 1978. He told the court that he did it so that women "could have some awareness of God."

Born Enrique Silberg in Cuba, he emigrated to the United States in search of "women, gold and God," he told his probation officer Richard Howell. He was obviously successful in finding himself because he went ahead and changed his name to the improbable moniker of Ubiquitous Perpetuity God.

Judge Lynn Taylor addressed the defendant as "Mr. God" throughout the hearing at Marin Superior Court. A court-appointed psychiatrist, Dr. Diane McEwen of Tiburon, said he suffered from a psychotic disorder. "God is simply too sick to be out in the streets," she said.

COLOR BLIND

Police in Rio de Janeiro were baffled when residents of the Parada de Lucas slum all came out at once on September 26 and painted all the buildings pale green. They suspected that the order came from local drug barons hoping to confuse the police, with obvious success.

TOOLS

•Richard Gardner, 23, was nailing up some molding at his mother-in-law's house in Lancaster, South Carolina, on Christmas night when he shot himself in the hand and his wife in the stomach. He had thought that the .25-caliber handgun he used as a makeshift hammer was empty.

•Sean Gale, 33, stopped for erratic driving outside Clonmel, southern Ireland, was found to be steering with a pair of pliers. "The steering wheel came off when we were visiting the mother-in-law," he told police.

WANTED—GOLDILOCKS

New York police are hunting a burglar who breaks into homes and makes porridge. He (or she) has struck ten times and never steals anything.

TUMBLED

Nashville, Tennessee, police were called to a laundromat after a cus-

VEGGIE SPECIALS

❤ French police are hunting a man who dresses up as a giant eggplant to rob banks. In the first heist in Marseilles the bank manager asked: "Are you serious?" "No, I'm an eggplant!" came the angry reply as the vegetable let off a shot. Staff handed over the cash. Before he left, the robber left a real eggplant on the counter. There have been three further raids by the eggplant.

❤ Chris P. Carrot's plan to campaign against animal cruelty dressed as a seven-foot carrot backfired when he visited a Texas school. The principal told children he was an example of why they must not talk to strangers.

❤ Izzie Rotterman, 81, and his business partner, Gloria Lepcio, 55, were entering a restaurant in Pompano Beach, Florida, on February 7 when a man jumped out of a car and grabbed Lepcio's purse. Rotterman beat the mugger over the head with a half-pound Vidalia onion, which he carried around because it was easier on his digestive tract than regular onions. The attacker fled empty handed.

tomer reported that a man had come in from the rain soaking wet, put a few coins in a dryer, climbed in, and was getting tumble-dried.

BIT OF A DING DONG

Do Trung Kien, deputy manager of a Vietnamese bank in Ho Chi Minh City, orchestrated a commando raid on the offices of Hai Yen Co., as the garment company owed the bank six billion dong ($574,000). Sixteen employees armed with high-velocity rifles snipped telephone lines and cordoned off the area. The bankers loaded three trucks with equipment pledged as collateral for the original loan before the police arrived and arrested them.

NATURAL STATE

In May of 1995, police investigated claims that smartly dressed men were stripping off their suits and dancing naked in the woods near Penn Common, England. Local residents had expressed worries about their children who play in the same area. "We just do not know what these men are up to," said Supt. Malcolm Gough. "We do not know whether they are genuine nudists, nature lovers, or if there are more sinister motives."

"It's been going, on and off, for about a year now, although it seems to stop after November," said resident Judy Bradburn. "People who have seen them say that all they wear are black shoes and black socks."

APPETITE SHARPENER

Doctors in the central Chinese province of Hunan are investigating a 32-year-old man who has eaten 1,320 pounds of glass in the past 17 years with no apparent ill effects. Ma Shuntian started eating glasses and beer bottles at the age of 15. Since then, he has devoured 1,700 glasses and 600 bottles. He married four years ago and for a while kept his habit a secret from his wife.

GOT A LIGHT?

Stefan Sigmond, 29, from Cluj in Transylvania, set a record in Bucharest on January 31 when he smoked 800 filter-tipped western cigarettes in less than six minutes through a special wheel-like device, breaking his 1995 record of 750. Last year he ate 29 boiled eggs in four minutes and—separately—jumped into a lake from a 135-foot-high platform. He will not, however, appear in the Guinness Book of Records, which now discourages gluttony and foolhardiness.

TWO LEFT FEET

Police in Hamilton, Ontario, found more than 1,000 shoes in a trash bin—all brand new, all Reeboks. And all, except one, for the left foot. Constable Mark Taylor said the shoes, sizes 9 through 11, include running shoes, hiking boots and sandals worth about $120,000 retail.

Officers suspect that the shoes were stolen and later discarded, but they haven't a clue why a thief wouldn't keep pairs. Perhaps some mischief was afoot.

DOUGH FOR BRAINS

As reported to Dick Kreck of the Denver Post third-hand, a woman visiting her in-laws in Aurora (either the one near Chicago or the one near Omaha, Nebraska), was crossing the parking lot of a grocery store when she noticed another woman seated behind the steering wheel of her car, clutching the back of her head. Asked if she was alright, she responded: "Yes."

Concerned, the first woman nevertheless called 911 and reported the encounter to police. When the cops arrived, they found the woman still sitting in the car, with her hands clasped behind her head. They asked if she were OK. "No," she said. "I've been shot." They asked her to take her hands down so they could see, but she replied that if she did her brains would fall out.

What police found when she lowered her hands was not her brains, but an uncooked biscuit stuck to her hair. A tube of biscuit dough in a grocery bag on the car's back seat had exploded, thwacking her with part of its contents. "This is a wonderful yarn," said a member of the Aurora Police Department. "The only problem is we cannot confirm ever answering such a call."

A slight variant of this tale was circulating on the Internet in May. The first woman's name was given as "Linda," the incident happened in Arkansas, and paramedics had to break into the locked car as the "victim" refused to let go of her head.

MAD MANACLERS

A woman from Wales, sunbathing on the cliffs in the center of Newquay, England, complained to two men that they were playing soccer too close to her. The men rushed towards her, snapped a lock around her ankle to which was attached a heavy ball and chain, and ran off. It had to be re-

moved by the fire brigade, using crash-rescue equipment and cutting gear.

OFF THE RAILS

A train crew made an emergency stop at Darien, Connecticut, at 2:30 a.m. as they thought they had run over a body. When they shone their flashlights on the track, a naked man, lying in the space between the rails, jumped up and attacked the three crew members before running off into nearby woods. One conductor was bitten twice on the leg and cut on his face while a second had a finger bitten. Artay Drinks, 23, of Bridgeport, was arrested about an hour later and booked on assault and trespassing charges.

MATH IS MURDER

A teacher at a middle school in Marepas, west of Paris, caused astonishment by asking her physics pupils the following question: "Hitler killed Jews by locking them in trucks whose exhaust pipe was connected to the inside. Knowing the volume of a bus is 50 cubic meters, what volume

PECULIAR PRESS

MAN FINED FOR QUACKING
Hong Kong Standard,
October 12, 1995

HUSBAND BITES WIFE'S "THING"
Monitor (Uganda), February 1, 1995

**MARRIAGE MASHED BY
MASHED SPUD MANIA**
Wolverhampton Express & Star,
May 3, 1995

of carbon monoxide must be given off to attain the mortal dose of five parts per 1,000? Knowing the victims took 20 minutes to die on average, what volume of carbon monoxide was produced hourly by the engine?"

JUST LAUNDER

Three South Africans posing as Liberian royalty were arrested in Johannesburg for trying to spend blackened paper they said would be revealed as American dollars if a chicken was slaughtered and its blood drunk. The trio claimed they had blackened $1.5 million to get it out of war-torn Liberia and tried to persuade a businessman that it would be his after he performed a ritual involving alcohol and chicken blood.

CEMENT SACRIFICE

The Longwan cement factory in Guangdong, China, ordered the entire workforce to attend a ceremony where a witch and a sorcerer sacri-

CROSS PURPOSES

Shinichiro Kaneko suffers for your home entertainment.

❦ Every Good Friday, the village of San Fernando in the Philippines holds a reenactment of Christ's crucifixion. Local Catholics allow themselves to be nailed to crosses for a few hours. This year, Shinichiro Kaneko from Japan asked to join the ceremony, in the hope that his suffering would persuade God to heal his critically ill younger brother. But Mr. Kaneko was not a believer and had no sick relatives; he is a pornographic actor specializing in sadomasochistic roles, and his crucifixion is to be released on video, much to the outrage of Filipino Christians.

❦ Fired cop Ricardo Chavez Garcia had himself tied to a cross outside Mexico City's U.S. embassy. He earned a summons for "illegal use of a police uniform" and did more to publicize his protest against police corruption than almost two months of quiet demonstration on the same spot.

❦ Fed up with music blasting at all hours from a bar below his apartment, Franco Moni of Rome staged a fake crucifixion on his home's balcony.

❦ Pupils at a Malawi nursery school nailed a three-year-old boy to a cross as he acted the part of Jesus Christ in a passion play. George Sembereka was freed only after a teacher heard his screams.

ficed a dog in an attempt to restore profitability to the plant, which lost 8 million yuan (over $950,000) last year. Workers and managers knelt down to ask for divine assistance, but shortly after the ceremony a power generator at the factory burned out.

LOAFER

Tatsumi Orimoto arrived in London in June and wandered the city's open spaces with baguettes strapped to his head. The Japanese artist, known as "Bread Head," has traveled the world for some time: He spent two years in Germany with a 9-foot chimney in his backpack, then a further five years crossing European roads with a cardboard box on his foot. In New York he spent a year dragging a cast-iron bathtub around Greenwich Village. "It's my way of communicating," he said.

WAIT IN VAIN

Claude Arcens, 47, has given up his daily vigil standing under the Eiffel Tower. In 1984, somebody dropped a purse which he found and kept. In the 12-year wait, all he collected was a lighter.

GREAT ESCAPES

•Like something out of a fairy tale, Maria Chavez escaped a Madrid prison by climbing down a wall on a 19-foot rope made from her own hair.
•A prisoner escaped from jail in Düsseldorf, Germany, by shipping himself in a cardboard box. Josef Schmid, 43, was in charge of mailing clothes made in the jail to a clothing warehouse. He hid the clothes, which were ready to be packed, climbed in the box and

YOU'RE GROUNDED!

❦ In Chieti, central Italy, a girl locked in a dark room for more than six years because she had a headache was freed by police in March. Carmela Borcheti was 16 when her uncle, a fortune-teller, decreed that the headache meant she was possessed by evil spirits and the only cure was to spend seven years in a dark room. Carmela's parents put her in her bedroom and fastened the shutters. Her ordeal ended when someone tipped off a social worker, who visited her home. Carmela, now 22, pale and thin and hardly able to stand, at first insisted that she did not want to leave her prison. "Go away," she told police. "I must lie here for six more months and then I can live again." Eventually, she was put on a special diet in a hospital's care. Her mother Maria, 49, and her father Francesco, a 62-year-old garbageman, were not charged since, under Italian law, they had committed no offense.

❦ The following month, police rescued a woman in northern Honduras who had been kept prisoner in a small, dark room by her mother for 18 years. She had been fed through a small hole. Maria Canales, 33, was seriously demented by the time a squad of 20 officers in the small town of Choloma raided the family home after being called by neighbors. The mother was charged with abuse and cruelty.

SCHWASCAR

THE SCHWASCAR AWARDS

TIMELY RESURRECTION

❧ Daphne Banks, 61, an epileptic, was pronounced dead at 2 a.m. on New Year's Day. At 6 a.m., minutes before she was to be placed in a mortuary refrigerator, undertaker Ken Davidson, a family friend, noticed a vein twitch in her right leg. Then he saw her chest moving up and down, and she began to snore. Meanwhile, the mortician was preparing a sealed body tray into which Mrs. Banks was to be placed and in which she would have suffocated. Mrs. Banks was rushed to intensive care, regained consciousness after 24 hours, and four days later was well enough to be transferred to a general ward. It later emerged that she had taken an overdose of epilepsy pills and sleeping tablets, which could have lowered her blood pressure so that her pulse was hard to find.

RUNNERS-UP

❧ On December 2, 1995, an 81-year-old Chinese woman, Xue Wangshi, stopped breathing and was sent to Tongshan county crematorium in Jiangsu province. As she was being moved along a conveyor belt into the furnace, she moved her right hand. The keen-sighted, alert crematorium attendants stopped the belt and she sat up.

❧ A beggar, pronounced dead at a hospital in Jammu, Kashmir, was taken to the local cremation ground, but was saved from a funeral pyre when mourners from another cremation noticed him moving.

❧ Medics had given up on heart attack victim Brenda Smith, 44, but they battled on when a nurse spotted a tear trickling down her cheek. They got her heart beating again 48 minutes later. "Clinically she was dead," said Dr. Suresh Chavda, one of the team who saved the mother of two at the Dallas–Fort Worth Medical Center in Texas. Mrs. Smith was unconscious for a week, but made a full recovery.

❧ In March, the body of suspected thief Mvuyisi Mcetywa was taken to a government mortuary in Umtata, South Africa. He regained consciousness just before he was to be refrigerated and lived to accuse three policemen of torturing him.

❧ If these stories frighten you, don't fear—help is on the way. Fabrizio Caselli, a Tuscan watchmaker, is marketing a special safety coffin for just under $5,000. If the "deceased" wakes up underground, he or she can activate a bleeping device. Also at hand will be a two-way microphone/speaker, a flashlight, a small oxygen tank and a heart stimulator. If sales are brisk, Caselli says that three emergency centers will be needed to respond to premature burial emergencies across Italy.

taped it shut from the inside. The next night at the warehouse, he cut himself free and made his getaway.

DOG TOLD ME TO

Robert Meier, of Tampa, Florida, accused of marrying his comatose girlfriend, Constance Sewell, hours before she died, then running up $20,000 on her credit cards, told police he knew it was wrong, but the woman's dog told him to do it. However, an investigator who searched the apartment said: "The dog was in the garage and didn't say anything."

ARTFUL ROGER

Roger Powell, 47, a former laborer from Porthcawl, Australia, is yours for £850,000 (about $1,360,000). He has been designated "a work of art" by Tony Kaye, a British artist-cum-phil-anthropist who now lives in Califor-nia. Kaye, once homeless himself, discovered Powell sleeping near Wa-terloo Station in London and per-suaded him to sign a contract guaranteeing him a home and living expenses for as long as he was pre-pared to be a work of art.

Kaye is hailed as the man who put "art" into TV commercials, and com-mands fees of up to $160,000 a day. He discovered Powell a year ago and has exhibited him outside galleries in America and France, including the Louvre and the Washington National Gallery, in a small steel frame in-scribed "Roger." Roger is to be ex-hibited in Moscow and Israel.

Powell visits Kaye's London office every Friday to pick up $120 ex-penses. His $95/week room in North London is paid for by the office. Both men assume the deal will last until one of them dies.

EYE CARAMBA!

❤ Dutch student Jim Terwiel, 26, was sentenced to 12 years in jail after a psychotherapist said he had confessed to using a crossbow to fire a ballpoint pen through his mother's eye, but an appeals court in The Hague dismissed the testimony and said the woman had died in a freak accident, falling with the pen in her hand.

❤ Cui Tingxun, a teacher in China's Shandong Province, was practicing the esoteric healing art of qigong with his wife when he suddenly attempted to gouge her eyes out, saying he had received instructions from a "greater being" to change her facial features. Cui then attacked his wife's jaw with his teeth, saying her mouth smelled bad, before finally decapitating her with a meat cleaver. Police found him holding the shoulders of his wife's torso, exhorting her to sprout a new head.

KERMITTED

A man aged 21 burst into a New Zealand radio station, took the man-ager hostage and demanded that the station play "Rainbow Connection" by Kermit the Frog. Wanganui police said the man was charged with kidnapping.

CULTS AND CONSPIRACIES

THE MOST EVIL POLITICIAN

David Griffiths was expelled from the Conservative Association in London after making a speech to an audience of two people in York House in August 1995. Among other outrageous views, he had urged that all criminals should be killed, all homosexuals should commit suicide, and those claiming social security benefits should gun each other down in the street.

In January, he announced that he was running as the Antichrist in the next general election. Griffiths, 35, who admits he was given a suspended sentence for assaulting a friend, claims to have known he was the Antichrist for some time, but kept it to himself for fear it would damage his political career. His campaign for the Twickenham seat (currently held by Conservative member of Parliament Toby Jessel) is being financed by a $55,000 legacy left to him in his parents' will. He is circulating a 44-page manifesto in an attempt to woo voters.

ECHOES OF THE PAST HAUNT TRAIN WRECK

On October 9, 1995, a passenger train was sabotaged in Hyder, Arizona, killing one of the crew and injuring more than 100 people. The FBI's attention was drawn to the Harney train disaster in Nevada on August 12, 1939, in which 24 people died. Both cases involved westbound trains, traveling at night through the desert on a track owned by the Southern Pacific Railroad. Both trains were derailed at the end of a bridge, both diverted into a stream bed. Both involved tricking the signaling system by maintaining an electric current between the two split rail ends. In both cases, the inside spikes were pulled from 11 ties. Photos of the two wrecks are all but indistinguishable.

The FBI found that two weeks before the Hyder crash a specialist railway magazine, the *Southern Pacific Tramline* published in Dunsmir, California, had run a detailed account of the 1939 sabotage, for which no one was ever arrested. They drew up a list of 30 subscribers in Arizona and asked all rail archives to report on any recent requests for information on the earlier case. At the time of the news reports, they had no firm leads, no witnesses and no suspects. Notes found near the scene, with a diatribe against the sieges at Waco and at Ruby Ridge, Idaho—both flashpoints in Militia folklore—signed by the "Sons of Gestapo," were thought to be a deliberate red herring. During the 1939 investigation, some suspicion was cast on Nazi sympathizers. This time, attention focused on disgruntled ex-employees of Amtrak. It planned to close part of the Southern Pacific line, with the prospect of heavy layoffs. The stretch of track where the Los Angeles–bound train was derailed was due to be abandoned in 1996.

KNEECAPS NABBED

Cultists raided dozens of tombs in a south Philippine province and stole kneecaps in the belief that they could be turned into amulets that protect against bullets. The raiders destroyed

25 tombs in two towns in Agusan del Sur on Easter Day in 1994. To maximize their effectiveness, the kneecaps have to be removed at the stroke of midnight Easter Day, according to a former cultist. The raiders were said to belong to two cults that police had enlisted in the fight against communist insurgency. One of these cults was called Tadtad ("Chop") after its reputation of chopping up and beheading some of its victims. Kneecap thieves were at it again in August 1995, but their alleged motive this time was quite different. Police in the central town of Bacolod investigated when residents in nearby Bago complained of hearing nocturnal hammering in a cemetery. Kneecaps were missing from 24 tombs. It was believed that they were ground into powder and burned like incense near a house burglars intended to rob. The smoke induces the occupants to sleep long enough for the looting to take place.

KIDS TODAY . . .

Young people in Littleton, Colorado, are using abandoned Titan missile complexes for Dungeons and Dragons games, cult animal sacrifices and orgies. They broke in with jackhammers and car jacks, allowing entry into the dangerous maze of tunnels, shafts and rooms below.

SATANCALIFRAGILISTIC

Massimo Introvigne, of the Italian Center for the Study of New Religions, announced that there was a secret agenda in the 1964 film Mary Poppins. Behind Mary's sweet-natured mask lay "a troubled creature bordering on the Satanic."

KENNEDY ASSASSIN FESSES UP

A man called James E. Files has "confessed" that he and the notorious Mafia hitman Charles "Chuck" Nicoletti crouched behind the grassy knoll in Dealey Plaza, Dallas, on November 22, 1963, and that both of them shot President Kennedy at the same time. He was paid $30,000 and was under orders not to hit Jackie Kennedy. Oswald was a decoy who never fired a shot; Nicoletti took his orders from Sam "Momo" Giancana who in turn answered to Anthony "Big Tuna" Accardo. Giancana, of course, is believed to have shared a mistress with the president. However, all three mobsters were murdered between 1975 and 1977, leaving no one to corroborate Files's story. Since Files is now serving a 50-year sentence in Illinois for the murder of a policeman, he has little to lose in confessing, while gaining his 15 minutes of fame. The FBI dismissed his story.

GREEN PARTY, BLACK MAGIC

Green Party activist Nicholas Galgani, 26, who believed himself the victim of a witches' coven, was found dead from multiple injuries at the base of a 300-foot cliff near his home in Lewes, England. A June inquest found that, shortly before his death, Galgani had been trying out some "magical practices" and was sent a voodoo doll and a cow's heart hammered through with nails. He had also told his girlfriend that he was having nightmares about a "black apparition." When detectives went to his apartment they discovered black crosses daubed across the doors.

Bible pages had been pasted on the walls, and foot-high painted letters pled: "Please God. Somebody save me. Protect me from black magic."

The police investigating Galgani's death were also examining a number of "unusual happenings" in Lewes, according to Detective Sergeant Bates, who said: "In recent weeks graves have been desecrated and cats killed and nailed to posts outside churches."

....

POLICE POSTPONE DOOMSDAY
....

About 150 policemen stormed a plantation in Malaysia's north Borneo state of Sabah, where about 200 followers of a doomsday cult had gathered to wait for the end of the world on September 28, 1994. The cult members were decked out in white robes and yellow amulets; some carried spears, long knives, bows and arrows and catapults. A few suffered cuts and bruises in the raid, but no one was seriously injured. Sabah's police comissioner, Maizan Shaari, denied a report that the cult had planned to carry out a human sacrifice. There were 192 arrests, including 40 women and 55 children. Almost all of them came from the predominantly Christian island of Timor, which is now under the yoke of the Indonesian regime in Jakarta. Sabah's palm plantations and construction industry have become a magnet for migrant workers from the Philippines and Indonesia.

LEGAL LUNACY

❦ Thomas Passmore of Norfolk, Virginia, cut off his hand because he thought it was possessed by the devil, then refused to let surgeons at Sentara Norfolk General Hospital reattach it. Now he is suing them for $3 million, saying they should have known he was crazy.

❦ Klaus Schmidt, 41, burst into a Berlin bank with a pistol and screamed, "Hand over the money!" Staff asked if he wanted a bag, to which he replied, "Damn right, it is a real gun." Guessing Schmidt was deaf, the manager set off the alarm. "It was ridiculously loud, but he didn't seem to notice." After five minutes, punctuated by Schmidt occasionally shouting, "I am a trained killer," police arrived and arrested him. Schmidt then sued the bank, accusing them of exploiting his disability.

❦ Factory worker Albert Fershurber, fired for oversleeping, took his boss to court—but failed to turn up for the hearing because he slept in.

❦ A disappointed sex-line caller, previously connected to a nagging wife instead of a panting girl, complained to trading standards watchdogs. The watchdogs said they couldn't take any action as the line was titled "Hear Me Moan."

❦ Rolf Lessinger, barred from building a house near Reisa in Germany, dug a huge crater, filled it with water and built a houseboat instead. The town has no planning laws for houseboats.

DEATHS AND SUICIDES

WHEN THE BOUGH BREAKS

Gunnar Larsen, 42, was carving his name on a giant oak in a high wind when a branch broke off, fell and crushed him to death in a public park in Herning, Denmark.

HARE AND GONE

A 72-year-old Dutch motorist hit a rabbit on the A6 freeway, north of Amsterdam. He pulled over at a services exit and was walking back up the road to attend to the stricken animal when he was run over and killed by a car coming from the opposite direction.

MYSTERY COMES OUT IN THE WASH

Les Horan, a washing machine mechanic, had dedicated 30 years of his life to a worldwide search for his father's World War II grave. Last summer, he was called out to a job at an apartment in Bromsgrove, England. Noticing a Royal Air Force plaque in the hall, he mentioned to the owner, Joe Grangier, that his father had also been an airman, and had been shot down over Akyab in Burma. He explained the difficulties he had experienced in tracing his father and said: "No one seems to have heard of Akyab."

It turns out that Grangier's unit had taken part in the 1945 invasion of Akyab Island, but he could recall no casualties. Horan explained that his father had been in the Royal New Zealand Air Force. His Sea Otter plane was shot down a couple of miles off the island by Japanese fighters on January 9, 1945. This was just one day after Grangier's arrival in Akyab.

Grangier then recalled that on the night of January 9, he went for a swim on Akyab beach and the body of John Horan was washed up with grievous wounds. It was buried in the civil cemetery, with Grangier in charge of the bearer party. Horan was later reinterred in the military cemetery in Rangoon.

After a lifetime's search involving trips to New Zealand, Les Horan had discovered the truth about his father two miles from his house.

POOR EXECUTION

Rita Quam was collecting rocks for her garden in Grand Junction, Colorado, when a man walked up in dark glasses, a black wig and a false mustache. He fired several shots from a semiautomatic pistol with a silencer, but they all missed. Then his gun jammed, so he tried to beat Quam on the head with large rocks. A policeman arrived and ordered the attacker to lie down; at this point he collapsed, his disguise fell off, and he had a fatal heart attack. Quam recognized him as Arthur R. Smith, a retired Chicago police officer and an old friend of her ex-husband, Howard.

MONEY WHERE YOUR MOUTH IS

A robbery suspect who tried to swallow some incriminating evidence choked to death on a $50 bill. The man collapsed in the back seat of a patrol car in Buffalo, New York, on April 25, 1995, about an hour after he was caught attacking a woman in a supermarket parking lot. Nine days earlier in Australia, Adam Kane Morris, a 23-year-old paranoid schizophrenic from Kew, Australia, had choked to death on a wad of ten $50 notes which he had swallowed during a fit in the bath.

LANDING FEAR

The body of a young man, 18 to 25 years old, was found floating in the Harbor Isle Marina in Island Park, Long Island, in the flight path to Kennedy Airport, on May 21. A homeowner reported hearing a loud boom, then a splash in the water, at 3:25 p.m. The victim carried Dominican currency and wore jeans that were not manufactured in the United States. An American Airlines jet touched down at Kennedy just three minutes after the splash, which occurred approximately when it lowered its landing gear at 2,000 feet.

Two days later, at 6:35 a.m., a boy cycling to school found a mangled body in the middle of a suburban street about eight and a half miles west-southwest of Miami International Airport. Neighbors had heard a thump, but didn't investigate. The body was covered in grease stains, suggesting that the man had stowed away in the nosewheel well of an airliner.

MAYBE IT'S YOUR PERSONALITY, PAL

A man aged 100, from Medan in Indonesia, who believed his 75-year-old wife was having an affair, killed her by cutting her throat after she refused to have sex with him.

BOOM TOWN

Attempting to blow yourself up can be a hazardous business—for your neighbors. Sergio Mazzaro tried the gas method and razed a three-story block of apartments in Bologna on March 9, 1996. At least four people were killed and several injured, but Mazzaro himself survived.

WHAT WERE THOSE TEN THINGIES AGAIN?

A man who lost an early-morning Bible-quoting contest killed the man who beat him. Gabel Taylor, 38, was shot once in the face outside his apartment in Dadeville, Alabama, on July 18. Police were searching for the suspect, who was thought to have left Dadeville. Taylor, a preacher's brother, and the suspect were comparing their Bible knowledge outside an apartment complex, each quoting different versions of the same passage. The suspect retrieved his Bible, realized he was wrong and threatened to kill Taylor, according to witnesses.

OUT OF SEASON

On Christmas Day 1994, Niyi Owoeye was driving his bus near Akure, capital of Nigeria's Ondo State, when he thought he saw an antelope at the side of the road. Fancying a snack, he drove at it and crushed it. Then he discovered that the "antelope" was really Mr. Ratimi Alesanmi, a member of the Federal Commission for Road Safety.

FLOSSED CAUSE

A laborer in Chon Buri, Thailand, got drunk, tied an aching tooth with a string to a pole and pulled it out without a painkiller. Unluckily, Cha, 40, bled to death, the alcohol having caused his blood pressure to soar.

WEATHER OR NOT, HE'S RESPONSIBLE

A mob killed Jim Motloutsi, 73, in the South African village of Mmatobole in Northern Province on January 18, 1996. They stoned him, doused him with gasoline, put a tire around his neck and set him ablaze. They held him responsible for the death of a woman aged 60 who had been killed by lightning in the village a week earlier.

DEAD DAD STARTS TREND

After Vo Lieu, 74, died of natural causes in Vietnam, his children administered a drug to his wife to prevent her screaming at the funeral; she died of a drug overdose before the funeral took place. A joint funeral was then held, but a truck transporting the coffins careered out of control and crashed into the funeral procession, killing a 26-year-old man and injuring six undertakers.

PLUMMING THE DEATHS

A peasant woman, boiling plums to make brandy in the Romanian village of Ruginoasa, died when the flames under her still set off a buried World War II shell.

COMPUTER ERROR

Accountant Arthur Roberts lost his temper when he accidentally wiped his firm's sales figures off his computer. He threw the machine out of his window in Brisbane, Australia— and killed pedestrian Peter Mulins. He was charged with manslaughter.

TAPE HEAD

Michael P. Olson, 13, was found dead by his uncle in the woods near his home in Eau Claire, Wisconsin. His entire head, including his mouth and nose, were wrapped in a large quantity of duct tape, and a roll of duct tape was found next to him. It was thought he had accidentally suffocated while experimenting with the tape. His family said he was obsessed with tape and had frequently wrapped GI Joe and Barbie dolls with it.

CAPPERS

❦ A 100th birthday party for Basilio Re in the small Italian village of Vigogna near Genoa ended abruptly when the wind blew off his hat and he slipped and died chasing it. He was found to have died of a heart attack.

❦ South African taxidermist Roelf Uys was celebrating his 33rd birthday in the bush in Northern Province when a hunter saw his hat bobbing in the long grass and, mistaking it for a pheasant, shot him dead.

THE REAPER RINGS TWICE

❦ A teenager who spent two months in a coma after she was knocked down by a car in November 1989 in Whitecairns, England, was killed on February 22 when she was hit by a truck at the same spot. Both accidents occurred when Gillian Sylvester, 19, crossed a main road to a bus stop opposite her house.

❦ Herman Lorenz, 88, was knocked down and killed by a train at a crossing in the Chicago suburb of Northbrook on January 13. Witnesses said he went round the crossing gates and kept going after the Amtrak train engineer sounded a warning horn. In October 1926, Lorenz survived a crash at the same crossing: a train sliced through the school bus he was riding and killed two people, including his seatmate.

❦ Ian Gamble, 16, was stabbed to death on February 24 after an argument with some youths as he walked through the grounds of England's Barnard Castle. A few yards away was a memorial to his brother, Darren, who was killed in an accident in March 1988, also at the age of 16. Darren and his friend Steven Laybourn were sitting in a car in the garage of Steven's home with the engine running to keep warm, but they fell asleep and were killed by the exhaust fumes.

❦ A man whose wife was killed two years ago in a snowmobiling accident was fatally injured himself when his snowmobile ran into a barbed-wire fence. Michael Staring, 35, of Pulaski, New York, died on February 18 when the sun's glare on the snow apparently caused him to misjudge the distance between the fence and an open gate. His wife died in January 1994 when her snowmobile was hit by a car.

❦ On November 8, 1995, Vittorio Veroni was killed on the Via Cartoccio level crossing in Remilia Emilia, Italy. His daughter Cristina, 19, had been killed four years earlier at the same crossing, by the same train, driven by the same driver.

FISH GAG

A Brazilian fisherman choked to death near the remote Amazon city of Belém after a fish unexpectedly jumped into his mouth. Nathon do Nascimento was fishing by the Maguari River, about 30 miles south of Belem, when the six-inch-long fish suddenly leapt out of the river and became lodged in Nascimento's throat while he was in the middle of a long yawn. Two other fishermen tried to help him, but by the time they arrived at the local hospital it was too late. "The fish obstructed his throat completely and he couldn't pull it out because he couldn't reach the tail," a doctor said.

STARDUST

In August, 1997, the ashes of 30 people, including *Star Trek* creator Gene Roddenberry and Timothy Leary, will be blasted into the stratosphere by the U.S. firm Celestis. For $5,000, the spaced-out send-off includes a commemorative video and the chance to orbit Earth for ten years before burning up.

TERROR IN PERU

The body of a 34-year-old woman with her heart, eyes, lungs and kidneys torn out, found in the Ucayali jungle in Peru, sparked a hunt for the feared "white man" who reputedly stalks the region seeking native Indian victims. In Andean legend, *pishtacos,* or devils that appear in the guise of foreigners, hunt and kill locals before stealing their body fat and organs to ship back to Europe for use in factories.

Alfredo Tananta, municipal official in the jungle village of Sharasmana, said that the murder had been preceded by the suspicious appearance of "strangers that looked like tourists, who, however, did not make contact with the locals," according to the local daily El Comercio. Other officials, however, believe the woman was killed by another local before being mauled by wild animals.

• A similar scare about child murder in Guatemala for the international organ trade [see FT76:48] appears to have abated. Last August, the United States lifted a two-and-a-half-year-old warning that recommended against non-essential travel to the country by U.S. citizens.

METHOD ACTING

An actor simulating a hanged man in the dungeon of a ruined 13th-century castle in Slovenska Lupca, central Slovakia, accidentally hanged himself. No one noticed that the 33-year-old man, who had tested the procedure several times previously, was dead until tourists pushed his body in fun as it dangled from a rope.

PEST CONTROL

A burglar died after he broke into a Los Angeles house that was being fumigated and was overcome by chemicals.

ZERO SUM GAME

Daniolo Maggioni, 38, shot a wild boar near his home in Varese, northern Italy. Searchers later found both the hunted and hunter dead—the enraged boar had attacked Maggioni and hurled him into a ravine before dying.

MEAT ME IN ST. PETERSBURG

✪ Ilshat Kuzikov, 35, was seized in his St. Petersburg apartment on August 23, 1995, after the severed heads of Misha Bochkov and Edik Vassilevsky had been found in nearby streets. There were two legs and arms in the hall and a casserole by the oven containing human bones, picked clean. A plastic bag hanging outside the window was filled with human flesh and onions. A shopping bag contained dried human ears and other parts, while there were many jars of pickled flesh which police referred to as "winter supplies." Kuzilov, a schizophrenic who'd been in and out of mental institutions, offered the investigators vodka and a meal if they let him go. "Ever tried human liver? It's really tasty," he said.

✪ Aleksandr Maslich, 23, and Aleksei Goluzov, 25, prisoners in the Alta region of Siberia, strangled another inmate, cut out his organs and cooked them in a washbowl over a blazing blanket and then ate them "to add some spice to their life." Imprisoned for an earlier triple murder, Maslich was sentenced to death in July 1995. Goluzov, in for robbery, got another 15 years. Both were declared sane.

In May, Maslich strangled his murderer cellmate with a blanket, cut out his liver and was caught trying to boil it over a fire made of rubber piping from a tap.

✪ A man in the Siberian town of Kemerovo confessed to killing a well-known criminal, Vladimir Laptin, and using his flesh as the filling for *pelmeni,* a Russian version of ravioli, which he shared with two drinking companions.

✪ A cannibal who ate his son and a drinking companion was committed to an asylum by a court in the Tula region of Moscow in March this year. The previous autumn, a man was arrested in Tula after biting the throat of a passerby.

✪ Yelena Dalonova, 76, was arrested on suspicion of killing her husband, then eating and canning his remains. Neighbors found the partial remains of Nikolai Dalonova, 83, on the stairs near the couple's apartment in Kaliningrad, outside Moscow. Cans of human flesh were found in the Dalonova's fridge.

✪ Two Ukrainian brothers were convicted of beating up a homeless man and beheading him with an axe. They cut flesh from the corpse, fried and ate it. The head was displayed in the home as a trophy. Anatoloy Novikov was sentenced to death and his brother Andriy jailed for 10 years.

✪ Gulnara Hinz stabbed her violent husband to death, baked his flesh in the oven and served it to members of his family at his birthday party in Uzbekistan. When relatives asked where he was, the 26-year-old woman told them they had just eaten him.

GENIUS AND DISCOVERY

YOU MUST REMEMBER THIS

Based on predictions of the rate of advances in microchip science, British Telecom's rather evocatively named Artificial Life team has suggested that, within as little as 30 years, it might become possible to store an individual's lifetime of memories on one chip—although BT is not currently funding any research in this area.

The basic idea behind the chip is essentially to create a device or set of devices that will perform a similar function to the "black box" flight recorders used in aviation. The devices could be attached to the optic, olfactory and auditory nerves, and record the electrical impulses exchanged between the sensory apparatus and the brain. Theoretically, these recorded impulses could then be played back later, or even implanted in another person's brain. The 30-year figure appears to have been arrived at by projecting the current rate of advance of microprocessor technology. It is estimated that we process more than seven quadrillion floppies of info over an 80-year lifespan.

Rather dramatically, the team has christened the concept "Soulcatcher." As the team conceives it, a recorder could be mounted on a wearable minicomputer, with probes attached to sensory areas of the brain. The probes would relay impulses to the chip, which would then record sights, sounds, smells, tastes and tactile sensations. Part of the system's elegance is that, as laid out at present, it would not require any specialized decoding apparatus; since the chip directly records electrical activity, it should be entirely possible to replay that activity straight into the brain, recreating precisely the original sensations. However, presumably some sort of decoder would have to be developed in order to allow mass viewing.

Many applications have been suggested for the chip. It could revolutionize law enforcement, allowing authorities to replay witnesses' and suspects' actual experiences of an alleged crime; this could, of course, place a potential weapon in the hands of totalitarian regimes. It has also been suggested that it could offer hope for people with Alzheimer's disease and other diseases that affect memory and other sensory functions.

HEAD RUSH

Present technology designed to help "read" thoughts has provided American scientists with the first pictures of a false memory. Researchers at Harvard University performed a series of experiments to induce false memories in their subjects. The subjects were read a list of related word-groups—for example, "cake," "sugar" and "chocolate," or "sharp," "thread" and "knitting"—and then asked to remember in which group each of another list of words came. Some of the words would be highly reminiscent of the words from the first list, but were not actually part of the list —"sweet," for example.

While all this was going on, the subjects' brains were photographed using a Positron Emission Tomography (PET) scanner. The PET process allows doctors to create detailed three-dimensional models of internal organs, even showing blood moving in vessels if required. The scans were used to construct models of the blood flow within the subjects' brains as they heard each word from the second list. If they remembered hearing a word, two areas of their brain would experience increased blood flow— the hippocampus and the left tempo-ral parietal area, which is where the brain deciphers sound patterns and recognizes words. However, when the "subject" merely thought they remembered a word, only the blood flow to the hippocampus increased.

WHERE DOES IT HURT?

In an attempt to combat repetitive stress injuries, American scientists have introduced voice-activated computers to sufferers of the disease; but some users of the machines experienced permanent sore throats. The problem was called "Repetitive Talk Injury."

NOSE PICKING IS SEXY

Two Wisconsin researchers have published the eagerly anticipated results of their exhaustive study of rhinotillexomania (nose-picking, to you and me). Research began in November 1991 when 1,200 citizens of Madison, Wisconsin, found a nose-picking questionnaire in their mailboxes. Among the survey findings: 66.4% of pickers did it "to relieve discomfort or itchiness" (versus 2.1% for "enjoyment" and 0.4% for "sexual stimulation"); 65.1% used the index finger (versus 20.2% little finger and 16.4% thumb); and "once removed, the nasal debris was examined, at least some of the time, by most respondents." Another triumph from the Department of Really Useful Applications of Your Taxes.

WATER POWER BAFFLES SCIENTISTS

Bottled mineral water was turned into fuel before an assortment of scientists and journalists in Baalbek, in Lebanon's

FAMILY WITH "GILLS"

Segundina Jimena claims that her three children, like her late husband, have "gills" and can stay underwater for six minutes, according to the Philippine newspaper the *Sun-Star Daily*.

The "gills" are small holes on the sides of the neck below each ear. Dr Antonio Yapha, chairman of the Cebu provincial health committee, planned to visit the family in Dumanjug, about 350 miles south of Manila. "If it is a congenital anomaly then I will convince them to see a pulmonary specialist," he said.

Mrs. Jimena said that she didn't know how to swim and that her children were just starting to learn. The family lives in a remote mountain village far from the sea. According to a TV report from Cebu, one of the children, Hipolito, said liquid passes through the holes whenever they drink. The holes enlarge when they go underwater, allegedly allowing them to stay submerged for up to six minutes.

Bizarre medical stories are very popular in the Philippines. In 1990 a woman claimed to have given birth to a fish, and in 1992 a man claimed to be pregnant.

eastern Bekaa Valley on October 31.

Three young men poured the water from a sealed bottle into a homemade machine composed of glass tubes, electric wires and a transformer usually used in making radio sets. After five minutes, the current that passed through the machine produced a half-water/half-gasoline liquid, some of which was poured on the ground and set ablaze and some of which was poured into the tank of a motorcycle, which was then taken for a spin.

Sheikh Khalil Shukair, the mufti of Baalbek, drank from the sealed mineral water bottles to ensure they had not been doctored and then checked the machine for traces of chemical elements. "I can assure you that there were no traces of gasoline or chemical elements in the machine. This is a great experiment," he said.

Mohammad Sherif, a physics professor at Baalbek High School, said: "There is no doubt water was changed into gasoline, although I don't know how they did it." One of the three men, self-taught electrician Abdo Ezzat Yaghi, said he had been working on the project for seven years.

The setting of the experiment was particularly appropriate, as many Lebanese Christians believe that Christ performed his first miracle, turning water into wine, in Qana, near the southern port of Tyre.

HEAD LINES

A skull thought to belong to Thomas Paine (author of *The Rights of Man*) is being genetically fingerprinted in Sydney, Australia, in an attempt to prove its identity. Researchers will try to match a fragment of the skull with DNA samples of a Sydney resident who claims to be a direct descendent of the 18th-century radical.

BIRTHDAY SURPRISE

❧ Natasha Tilsley, 18, of Lanner, England, mistook her pregnancy for constipation. She had the surprise of her life when she gave birth to a baby girl after drinking a glass of liver salts. In a state of shock, she wrapped the baby in a towel and put her in the garden shed with a light left on. Her father found the baby the next day after he heard her crying. The night before the birth, Natasha had worked as a waitress until midnight and six weeks earlier she was modeling swimsuits. She remained a size eight right up to the birth.

❧ Amanda Galloway, 23, of Kitts Green, England, saw her doctor with a backache and was astonished to be told that she was in labor. Hours later, the unexpectant mother was in the hospital clutching an eight-pound, eleven-ounce boy who she named Ryan.

❧ Pauline Stone, 37, who runs the Vittoria pub in Clifton, England, flew to Cuba for a second honeymoon with her husband Philip three days after she discovered she was pregnant. She thought she had carried the baby for only a few weeks as she had not put on much weight; but two days later she gave birth to Margaret, a four-pound, six-ounce baby girl.

THE SCHWASCAR AWARDS

SNAIL MAIL

☜ In July 1994, Walter Mason, 74, received a letter from his fiancée Vera posted in Hull, England, on February 5, 1942. Walter was in the Royal Naval Voluntary Reserve, and the letter followed him through the Russian and Atlantic convoys, the North African campaign, the evacuation of Greece and even to Tokyo. It never caught up with him and ended up in the Royal Navy's mail office, where Ray Osgerby, one of Walter's old shipmates, found it in 1986. Vera, who had been Walter's wife since March 1942, had just died, so Mr. Osgerby put it aside and rediscovered it eight years later. When Walter finally got it, he was so moved it took him a week to pluck up the courage to open it.

RUNNERS-UP

☜ A parcel containing a book of sales tips from the National Salesman Training Association in Chicago was sent to Jim Post in Windsor, Ontario, in 1934, but disappeared into postal limbo for 62 years. Mr. Post was 105 years old when he received the book in January, 1996.

☜ A letter meant to go from one side of Felixstowe, England, to the other in 1991 first went to Felixton in South Africa, then to Felixtow in South Australia before arriving at the correct address a mile or two from where it was sent. The 25,000-mile round trip took a mere three months.

☜ Delayed for 44 years: a letter to retired Chicago steelworker Tommy Klyczec from his girlfriend, Martha, saying she loved him. "I thought she didn't want to marry me," he said. By the time he got the letter he was 62 and married for the second time.

☜ A 1964 letter from Emily Smith to her mother Mary Warner, on holiday near Salisbury, England, was returned to the sender in 1994 with a demand for 50 cents extra postage.

☜ This year, a 1971 letter written by six-year-old Marina Cuboni to Santa Claus was returned by the Italian post office to her mother's house in Sardinia with "Addressee unknown" on the envelope.

☜ Five opened and empty envelopes sent from Sweden, France, Korea, Pennsylvania and California were delivered to Willard Nicholson's New Jersey motorcycle accessory business 19 years late. They came with a message from the Postal Service that "an occasional mishap" will happen.

☜ In June 1987, Antonia Hatzakis in Chania, Crete, wrote to her boyfriend Manolis Hatzakis, working in Heraklion 60 miles away, that she was pregnant. The letter arrived in January 1994 and was opened by her six-year-old son—the couple had been married and had the baby.

HOAXES AND PANICS

VOLCANO PANIC

A radio reporter in the small Filipino city of Lucena said he had just received news that Banahaw, the nearby volcano, was going to erupt. Thousands fled their homes and two people died from heart attacks. Police later said it was a hoax by unidentified "amateurs." Banahaw's last known eruption was in 1743.

SHADES OF ORSON WELLES

Tenants in an apartment block in the Philippines city of Baguio panicked when a tenant spread the word that an international satellite television network had reported asteroids falling on Mongolia, China and Spain, killing millions. The "report" was really a movie, *Without Warning,* which tells the story of an asteroid shower in the form of news broadcasts.

TAKE ME TO YOUR BEDROOM

Balding and pale with thick glasses, no one would have believed that 59-year-old Barry Briskman was an extraterrestrial—except for three young girls. He was, however, an all too human man with a mission: to have sex with under-age girls. Pretending to be from another planet was his tactic.

Briskman, from planet Los Angeles, was already serving a 10-year sentence in Nevada for seducing a 12-year-old girl with this trick when he was sentenced to another 20 years for "assaulting" two 13-year-old girls in the Tropicana Hotel, Las Vegas. Briskman told the girls, all runaways, that he was from Cablell, an all-caucasian planet ruled by Queen Hiternia, and was currently ensconced in the Tropicana penthouse, having parked his spaceship at Lake Tahoe. He painted a picture of a wonderful world in which the unhappy girls could do whatever they wanted. "He would let them drink and smoke cigarettes—they thought he was cool," said prosecutor Steven Ipsen.

He said he had to recruit a team of females of superior beauty and intelligence to take back to Cablell; but first, he told the girls, he had to break down their "sub-cons" (subconscious intelligence barriers) in order to double their IQs. This involved a superior Hiternian process that would appear to earthlings to be very similar to strip-poker after a few drinks. The girls were still not ready for space travel; they had to acquire special immunities (that he called IRFs) to space diseases—and the quickest way known to wise spacefolk of acquiring these IRFs was through sexual intercourse. After each session of "injections," Briskman would appear to phone "Andy," the Cablellian master computer Andrak 4000, which confirmed the girls' new IRF rating.

The offenses occurred in 1990 and came to light when the family of one girl went to the police. "He's a classic pedophile," said Detective John Vannerson of the Los Angeles Police Department's unit investigating the sexual exploitation of children. "He spins a magical, seductive tale." One victim, a former child actress who is now 18, conceded: "He led me to believe many things. I wanted to believe them. He manipulated us . . . I didn't know I was going to have sex with him when I started. He started out gradually. It was a team. We were going to be the best of friends."

One girl in court said she wanted to forget and move on, admitting: "I don't feel I was the smartest of people for going along." The other sobbed bitterly: "He's a gross, perverted, hairy old man and he makes me so sick. I trusted him as a father figure and he betrayed that trust."

HUSBAND HACKING SHAM

A Hong Kong court convicted Sham Kwok-keung, a former policeman, of "unlawful sex acts by false pretenses." Mr. Sham enjoyed coitus with a 41-year-old woman after posing as a doctor to convince her that having sex with him was the only possible way to prevent other doctors from chopping off her husband's penis.

UNWELCOME WAGON

When Tom Hutchins cleaned out the basement of his new home in Westminster, Vermont, in September 1994, he came upon some crates left by a pilot who owned the place before him.

Two days later, he was cutting his lawn and wondering why so many planes were circling the southern Vermont hills. Then his lawn started to fill with men in combat fatigues and carrying radios.

When he moved one of the crates in his basement, Hutchins had unwittingly triggered an aircraft distress beacon inside it. More than 100 rescuers from the Air Force, the Rhode Island Civil Air Patrol and other

agencies were assigned to track the source of the signal. Their directional finders finally led them to Hutchins's basement, where they turned off the battery-powered beacon.

All aircraft are required to carry the cigarette pack–sized devices, but pilots are supposed to remove the batteries when they are not in the aircraft. Hutchins faced no punishment, but was likely to get a nasty letter from the federal government.

BILKING BIRDBRAINS

Birdkeeper Tony Sutton, of Woodley, England, launched a public fund-raising appeal to provide Musket, a European eagle owl, with a contact lens. He claimed that it was blind in one eye after being pecked by other fledglings. Bird lovers were asked to donate $1,875 to the Woodley Wildlife Center in Berkshire care of Barclays Bank. But the wildlife center didn't exist and Sutton was arrested on deception charges.

WHEN GONADS ARE GONERS

Mobs in Cameroon have hanged three men accused of using evil powers to cause male genitals to disappear merely by shaking hands. Several other "penis-snatchers" were in hospital after being badly beaten, according to the *Cameroon Post*. The incidents were reported in the towns of Limbe, Tiko, Muea and Batoke, all on the Atlantic sea route between Cameroon and neighboring Nigeria; most of the alleged snatchers were Nigerian. An 18-year-old student said that, when he shook hands with a Nigerian friend, "he felt an electric-like current run through him, and a feeling that his manhood had retreated into his stomach." Doctors said that all the "missing" genitals were unharmed and normal.

An earlier wave of missing member rumors swept through Nigeria in 1990 and Uganda. These rumors bear some resemblance to the shrinking penis panic known as *koro* in Malaysia and *shook yang* in China.

DUD

Policeman Terry Chard, 30, was dispatched to guard a black metal "land mine" that washed up on Whitecliffe Bay beach on the Isle of Wight, England. He stood guard for five hours in the pouring rain before being told by bomb disposal experts that it was a drain cover.

FLIGHTS OF FANCY

Ted Joffe, general manager of American Minerals Inc., was stopped by Osaka airport police after the crew of his Thai Airways International flight from Manila on August 4, 1995, reported that he had refused his meal, "which could indicate that he swallowed drugs to smuggle into Japan." A bemused Mr. Joffe was soon released. "Next time I'll stuff the meal into the seat pocket in front of me," he said.

BAG O' WIFE

Police pounced on an elderly man when they raided a pub in Loughborough, Lincolnshire, after a tip-off about a drug dealer. The elderly suspect then explained that his bag of white powder was the ashes of his late wife Alice, which he carried everywhere.

SO STUPID IT'S CRIMINAL

❦ A desperate prisoner spent two days covering his body in yellow highlighter to fake a bad case of jaundice. His plan—to escape on the way to a hospital—was thwarted when a night guard saw him using the pen on his face. "He had carefully painted his whole body, even his private bits," said a spokesman for the Isle of Wight Prison in England.

❦ Two bank robbers in Washington, D.C., ditched face masks and rubbed lemon juice into their faces instead because they'd been told it blurred security cameras. It didn't work, of course; they were arrested and jailed for 24 years.

❦ A thief looking for a free suntan has been scarred for life. The man walked into a Salisbury, England, hospital on May 29 and stole doctors' pagers and a white coat. Then he spotted the vertical sunbed, stripped off his clothes and set the machine for a 45-minute session—almost 300 times the recommended dose. When his sunburn erupted into all-over blisters, he took himself to another hospital 20 miles away, where staff had him arrested.

❦ Steve Larking, 18, charged with breaking into a nudist camp in Whiston, England, was arrested after a finger found in a chain link fence was sent for prints.

INEPTITUDE AND STUPIDITY

CLEANED OUT

Robert Keeler of Harrisburg, Pennsylvania, used his shop vacuum to draw gasoline from his car's tank. Sparks ignited the fuel, sending flames 30 feet into the air. The car was destroyed, as well as his newly renovated $200,000 house. Keeler was unhurt.

DUMMIES

Official figures suggested that 78 people died when the Pasar Anyar shopping center in Bogor, West Java, was gutted by fire on March 28, 1996. Forensic examination, however, showed that only ten had died; the rest of the victims were charred shop mannequins and a cat.

RADIO GAGA

Astronomers using the radio telescope at Parkes Observatory in Australia thought they had important evidence of alien life when they picked up a distinctive radio signal at 2.3 to 2.4 gigahertz every evening about dinner time. They later discovered that the signal was coming from the microwave oven downstairs.

NAKED AS A JAILBIRD

For more than two months, Ms. Sydney Samuel Mitchell was lodged in the men's dormitory of DeKalb County Jail in Decatur, Georgia—despite undergoing a strip search. When brought in on car theft charges, the 5-foot-11-inch,

235-pound Mitchell was taken to the male booking area and made no attempt to correct the misidentification. The officer who conducted the search observed chest hair, some facial hair, and no indication that Mitchell was a woman. Her true gender also went unnoticed in the jail's semi-private showers. The gender error came to light when a pre-trial coordinator repeatedly referred to Mitchell with male pronouns during an interview with her parents.

BYEWATCH

Lorenzo Trippi, a lifeguard in Ravenna, Italy, lost his job when three people drowned after he had hit them with life preservers. Police said his aim was too accurate.

STRONGARMED

Seven Spanish teenagers were hospitalized after trying to mug a defenseless woman in Alicante. Herminia Alvarez, as the boys discovered, is a circus weightlifter, the centerpiece of whose act is supporting eight people on one shoulder.

FUNERAL FOLLIES

•More than 50 relatives and friends of Tom Galligan paid their last respects at a cremation service in Cardiff, Wales. Seventeen days later, it was discovered that the body in the coffin was that of another corpse from the the University of Wales Hospital, John Callaghan, 76. By the time the mix-up was caught, Mr. Galligan's relatives had unknowingly scattered Mr. Callaghan's ashes. The family will now have to go through a second cremation for Mr. Galligan; luck is even worse for the late Mr. Callaghan, who wished to be buried.

•A funeral service in Gravesend, England, ended with Rod Stewart singing the line: "If you want my body, and you think I'm sexy." Curate Andrew Williams, who installed the sound system in All Saints Church, forgot to erase the tape which had just played the deceased's request, *Nessun Dorma.*

DIE HARDS

☻ Huang Pin-Jen, a 27-year-old Taiwanese soldier, and his 26-year-old transvestite boyfriend Chang Shu-Mei, decided to commit suicide together because both sets of parents were opposed to their relationship. They stuck their heads in plastic bags for an afternoon, but this only caused them to vomit. Then they decided to drive their car off the Central Cross-Island Highway, but they missed the water and ended up unharmed in a valley.

On April 21 they rented a room on the 12th floor of the Samantha Hotel in Taipei. They tried hanging themselves with nooses made from bedsheets tied to ceiling rods, but when they jumped they brought the ceiling down. So they tried the gas fire, but were sick again and passed out. The meter ran out and they woke up with headaches. Then they jumped out of the window hand-in-hand, but crashed through the tin roof of a five-story restaurant below, wrecking a lobster tank and ending up on a banquet table. They were both hospitalized in Kaohsiung with fractures but in a stable condition.

☻ Distraught over eye problems, a 69-year-old man from San Mateo, California, tried five methods of suicide on August 3, 1994. He slashed his wrists, stabbed himself in the stomach with a 12-inch knife, tried to drown himself, took an overdose of Tylenol and jumped from his first-story window with a clothesline tied around his neck. The rope broke. Then he decided he wanted to live and called 911 for help.

☻ When his wife left him, Alan Urwin, a 46-year-old ex-miner from Sunderland, England, made seven attempts to end it all in the space of three months. Having survived three drug overdoses, he wound an electric wire around his body, got into a bath and plugged in. The fuse blew and he suffered a minor electric shock. He then used the same length of wire to tie a hangman's noose around his neck, but the wire snapped and he fell, very much alive, to the floor.

For his sixth effort on August 11, he broke a gas pipe in his bedroom and lay next to it. When this didn't kill him, he lit a match. The explosion blew away the gable end of his semidetached house, along with the windows and part of the roof. He was pulled from the wreckage with nothing worse than flash burns. A year later, he was a considerably more cheerful man and was on speaking terms with his wife.

DEAD WRONG

❦ Ajay Chopra, 34, known to his friends as "Happy," went missing from his home in New Delhi about two monsoons ago. The family searched for him in vain. On the evening of July 19, 1995, Ajay's brother Ashok, returning from work, thought he saw Ajay at the Jamuna Bazaar. He walked up and asked the man if he was Happy, and on receiving an apparent affirmative in

Ashok embraces his brother Happy, who didn't die and wasn't cremated.

the way of a nod, brought him home. Ajay, his elder brother observed, hadn't eaten for some time. He was not surprised at his inability to respond to queries as Ajay was known to be a drug addict. Ashok bathed and fed his brother, but before he had a chance to talk to him, the man just rolled over and died. Grief-stricken friends and relatives gathered and on Thursday morning the body was taken to Nigam Bodh Ghat and cremated.

In the evening, Ajay strolled back home after a pilgrimage to Vaishno Devi and Hardwar, unaware that he had missed his own cremation that morning. So who was the dead man? The heap of ashes offered no clue for the police. "The resemblance was uncanny," said Ashok. "Not only myself, but the whole neighborhood thought Ajay had come back."

A huge crowd thronged their residence at Shora Kothi on the Friday morning, eager to catch a glimpse of the man who had risen from his ashes and had by then become a demigod. "People started touching Happy's feet, seeking his blessings and offering him money," said Ashok.

❦ Early in the morning of December 17, 1993, the body of a man was found in a sports park in Hino, a district of western Tokyo. He had frozen to death. Neighbors told police he resembled a 45-year-old local man, whose older brother lived nearby. The police went to the man's house and discovered that the younger brother had indeed been missing for three days. The distraught elder brother duly identified the corpse, the police passed it into his custody and he arranged a cremation the follow-ing day, according to Japanese custom. The day after that, the younger brother returned home and was stunned to hear of his premature death. The brothers shamefacedly returned to the police station. There is a Japanese saying that somewhere in the world there are three people who resemble you exactly. "The dead man was clearly one of the three who looked like the brother," said a local police officer. "His face, height and physique were just the same. It has been 38 years since I began working as a policeman and it is the first time I have come across such a mistake."

ANTIQUITIES

BUDDHA'S BIRTHPLACE REVELATION

According to legend, Prince Gautama Siddhartha, the founder of Buddhism, was born under a banyan tree in Lumbini on the Nepali-Bihar border, 200 miles southwest of Katmandu. An inscribed stone pillar erected by Asoka, the Buddhist emperor of India, marks the spot.

In February, the Nepalese prime minister announced that two years of excavations by archeologists from six countries had confirmed the legend. The area excavated is spread over three square miles of gardens, including a pond where Buddha's mother, Maya Devi, is believed to have bathed before walking 25 paces to the spot where she gave birth. The birthplace was discovered in May 1995 under a temple honoring Maya Devi, but there was no announcement until studies were complete. According to Buddhist annals, Asoka placed a stone on top of bricks at the birthplace, and this was found, about 25 paces from the aforementioned pond. Artifacts including coins, terracotta figurines and pottery earlier than the Mauryan period (321 B.C.) were unearthed in a series of 15 chambers. The project to find the birthplace was inaugurated in 1967 by the UN secretary general, U Thant, a Burmese Buddhist.

Gautama was born around 623 B.C. and his birthplace was marked by Asoka, the third Mauryan emperor (274–236 B.C.) in 249 B.C. during a pilgrimage to all the sites associated with his life.

FIRST CALL

Traces of retsina found in a jar fragment dating from 5400–5000 B.C. has pushed back the date of the earliest proven use of alcohol by some 2,000 years.

STEEL WORKS

Archaeologist Gill Juleff has unearthed and relit a legendary high quality steel-making plant that operated more than 1,000 years ago. The "incredibly efficient" ancient plant at Samanalawewa, Sri Lanka, which used conduits to harness windpower, produced results comparable to direct smelting—a technique "discovered" in Europe a millenium later. "It was not only possible, it was exceptionally simple."

CHARLESFORT FOUND

The site of the first attempt at a European colony in the United States may have been discovered. Pieces of 16th-century French pottery are said to prove that the colony of Charlesfort lies beneath a golf course on the U.S. Marine base at Parris Island, near Beaufort, South Carolina.

The colony was built by an expedition of 150 Huguenots, led by Jean Ribaut, which landed in May 1562, about 20 years before the first English settlement at Roanoke, Virginia. As soon as the tiny fort was built, Ribaut returned to France for fresh supplies and more settlers, leaving behind a garrison of 27 men. He promised to be back within six months, but was diverted to England by civil war in France and was jailed as a Huguenot spy. At Charlesfort, fire destroyed most of the supplies, the men rebelled and killed their commanding officer, and about eleven months after the settlement was started, the mutineers sailed for France. The colony was recorded by both the French and the Spanish, but had apparently disappeared without trace. The Spanish established their first colony at St. Augustine, Florida, in 1565 and a year later built Santa Elana in South Carolina. Dr. Chester DePlatter and Stanley South, archeologists at the University of South Carolina, were excavating Santa Elana when they realized that archaeological and documentary evidence pointed to Charlesfort being on the same site. After the French settlers had abandoned Charlesfort, only a servant boy, Ruffi, who had taken refuge with the Indians, stayed behind. It was he who led the Spanish to the site of the fort, where they used the moat and foundations to start their own settlement.

THE RABBIT AND THE CRAB

In 1054, a supernova explosion created the Crab Nebula, visible by day for some 23 days according to contemporary Chinese astronomers. Archeologists recently discovered a plate from the Mimbre culture that depicts a rabbit shaking an object with its hind paws. Robert Robbins, an archaeologist at the University of Texas, has suggested that this image represents the birth of the Crab Nebula. The rabbit is a lunar symbol in Mimbrean mythology and the object held between its paws seems to be a star with 23 rays, the same number of days

the supernova was visible. The Indians probably interpreted it as the Moon trying to get rid of a rival and, after about three weeks, winning the fight.

SHROUD IN CONTROVERSY

At a meeting of the American Society of Microbiology held in New Orleans on May 21, 1996, Dr. Leoncio Garza-Valdes and Professor Stephen J. Mattingly of the University of Texas Science Health Center at San Antonio asserted that the Shroud of Turin is many centuries older than the 1262–1384 indicated by the 1988 carbon tests. Working with British and German scientists, the Americans say that a film of bacteria and fungi on the linen threads might have skewed the dating; the only evidence presented for this thesis was that linen wrappings on an Egyptian ibis mummy tested 550 years younger than material from the bones. Nothing can be proved until a technique is developed for separating the film from the fiber.

ICONOCLAST SEEKS JOB

In June, Monsignore Guillermo Schulenburg Prado, abbot of the Basilica of Guadalupe, Mexico's holiest shrine to the revered Virgin of Guadalupe, made an unpopular announcement. He said that the story of the Virgin's appearance in 1531 before an Aztec peasant named Juan Diego was not a historical event but "a symbol." Diego was beatified by the present Pope in 1990. Prado was immediately denounced by a chorus of Mexican bishops, who called for his resignation and a Vatican inquiry. Some suggested he was senile. The miraculous image of the Virgin of Guadalupe on Juan Diego's cloak has been venerated for more than four centuries and became a powerful icon in the war of independence against Spain. A recent poll showed that 78 percent of Mexican Catholics have a reproduction of the image in their homes.

DIRTY LAUNDRY

Pilgrims flock to see the seamless robe allegedly worn by Christ.

❦ The seamless robe, or Holy Tunic, believed to have been worn by Jesus on his way to Calvary, was put on display for four weeks in a sealed glass case in the Trier, Germany, cathedral. From its cut, the garment does not look like a robe, and certainly not one from Christ's time and wardrobe. It is more like a liturgical garment from relatively recent times. At some point, silk and taffeta adornments were added to the original fabric and the whole thing was dipped into a preservative rubber solution, rendering it impervious to carbon dating. The end result is a rigid material like canvas or felt with the smell of burning tires. Textile historians say it is impossible to verify its authenticity.

❦ Robe skeptics in Trier exhibited a pair of longjohns which they claimed had belonged to Karl Marx, the city's most famous son, in an art gallery directly opposite the cathedral's giant refreshment tent. The venerable underwear dangled in a halo made of wedge-shaped pieces of wood, atop a three-winged altar. A journalist asked the altar's creator, local artist Helmut Schwickerath, if the relic was genuine. "Of course," he replied, struggling to maintain a straight face. The longjohns now belong to the Committee from the Preservation of Anti-Capitalist Artifacts, a group serious enough to be even more outraged than the local archbishop about the artist's presentation.

POLITICAL ASYLUM

❦ When the Russian psychic and hypnotist Anatoly Kashpirovsky lost his parliamentary seat, he warned that he would use his psychic powers to render impotent anyone trying to evict him from his government apartment.

❦ Dendler, head of the Ulm Theatre in der Westentache, is set to become personal jester of German president Roman Herzog. Dendler says Herzog agreed after many requests.

❦ When questioned by local journalists last October about France's resumption of South Pacific nuclear tests, the French ambassador to New Zealand, Jacques Le Blanc, said a 110-kiloton bomb was technically not a bomb because it was exploded underground and did not produce a mushroom cloud. Rather, Le Blanc said: "It is a device which is exploding."

❦ Saint Barbara, a 4th-century martyr, has been made patron saint of Russia's intercontinental nuclear missile force. Patriarch Alexei II said he chose this saint because her feast day (December 17) was the same as Russia's official Rocket Forces Day.

❦ Kidnappers in Bogotá holding the brother of former president Cesar Gaviria have demanded that Gabriel García Márquez, the Nobel Prize winning novelist, assume Colombia's presidency. The demand came in a communiqué issued by the shadowy group known as Dignity for Colombia.

❦ The star speaker of a British Council seminar on "How Can Democracy by Sustained?", Brigadier Julius Maada Bio of Sierra Leone, was unable to attend, as he had just overthrown his country's government in an army coup. His first decree: to cancel the forthcoming elections.

SHOE-IN

An early medieval shoe fragment has been discovered in a sack bought from a gardening center. The bag of peat was destined for flower pots until Tom and Rona Gibson from Topsham, England, came upon the ten-inch-long piece of leather. They took it to the Royal Albert Memorial Museum in Exeter, where its was dated at A.D. 800–1200.

HURRIAN HOME

Giorgio Buccellati believes he has found Urkesh, the home of the Hurrians (or Horites), a people said to have ruled a rich Middle Eastern kingdom about 4,000 years ago. A single reference appears in the Old Testament and another appears on an Egyptian clay tablet from 2000 B.C. After eight years of excavations, Buccellati and his colleagues believe the site is the town of Tell Mozan in Syria, 400 miles northeast of Damascus. Agatha Christie and her archaeologist husband Max Mallowan had explored the same area on a hunch, but gave up after two days of digging.

Artifacts indicate that the women of Urkesh had well-established property rights and that the crown prince was remarkably ugly.

COINING IT

Four 1,500-year-old coins from the early Byzantine empire were discovered in a Chinese tomb belonging to the northern dynasties (A.D. 386 to A.D. 581) in the northwestern Ningxia region. The gold coins reflect a history of cultural exchange between ancient China and Rome, and are the first of their kind to be found in China.

The
Animal
World

THE ANIMAL WORLD

From the Nessie wannabee six-foot conger eel in Loch Long, Scotland, that gave a diving instructor a run for his oxygen, to the New Hampshire Irish setter who saved its owner's life by dialing 911—if it kidnaps poodles, listens to its master's voice, or merely surfaces on occasion, it's a creature that we will feature in this petting zoo cum freak show.

Natural born weirdness was well up this year chiefly due to two factors: the remarkable stream of new species discovered in the Vu Ang Nature Reserve in Vietnam, and the genuinely astonishing level of international interest in the Goatsucker, the mystery "manimal" that rampaged through Puerto Rico and beyond, attacking farm animals. Out-of-Place Animals and Attacks on Animals were up while Attacks by Animals held fast. Old standbys Water Monsters and large hairy loner types were up, with several sightings of Nessie (the real McCoy) and Bigfoot through the year.

OUT-OF-PLACE ANIMALS

SHOCKOLI

Janet Pillow bought a bag of broccoli at a Whitstable, England, supermarket and sliced a large, poisonous, seven-inch Spanish water viper in half when she opened it. This happened on June 19, part of England's National Broccoli Week.

RAINING CATS AND CATS

An enterprising vicar whose cat had gotten stuck in a tree was unable to reach it by ladder. So he attached one end of a rope to the branch on which the cat was stuck and the other end to his car bumper, then drove away slowly, thus lowering the branch so that the cat could jump down. But the rope snapped and the unlucky cat was suddenly propelled heavenwards.

Meanwhile, a mother and daughter were picnicking on their lawn nearby. The girl said: "Mommy, I'd like to have a cat."

"You'll have to ask Jesus for one," said Mom. At this point, the flying feline came hurtling through the air and landed on the lawn. It has stayed with them ever since. If this yarn sounds off-the-wall, it should be

pointed out that the tale has very respectable pedigree indeed. It comes from the church magazine of St. John with St. Michael in Bournemouth, England, via the *Poole Advertiser*.

RECTAL RODENT

An ostensibly genuine version of the gerbil yarn appeared in the *BMA Journal* in May. Devito Bistone got a live gerbil stuck in his ascending colon. Koko Rodriguez attempted to rescue the animal with a cardboard cylinder, then lit a match "to improve visibility." A methane combustion occurred. Bistone was treated for "partial thickness burns of the natal cleft" at Salt Lake City General Hospital, Utah. Rodriguez suffered a singed mustache and a broken nose. The gerbil survived.

SOFA, SO GOOD

In Edmonton, Alberta, a hamster lost and believed dead for two years and four months turned up alive, well and living in the sofa. Hammie apparently carved a hole in the stuffing, lived off scraps left by the family's other pets and snuck out at night to drink from the cat's water dish. Owner Cathy Cummins said the family had moved twice since Hammie disappeared.

TRAINED PIGEONS

According to a number of people writing to the *New Scientist*, pigeons are catching underground trains to save flying time across London. The letters were triggered when Rachel

PECULIAR PRESS

LIONS ELECT NEW DISTRICT GOVERNOR
Irish Times, July 21, 1995

DEER CONGRESS TO BE HELD IN CORK
Irish Times, July 13, 1995

GUINEA-PIG JUDGE QUITS
Sunday Express,
August 27, 1995

SURVIVORS

This king of beasts still rules.

❧ South African animal specialist Hym Ebedes has discovered eleven lions at a forgotten zoo in Addis Ababa, Ethiopia, that bear a striking resemblance to biblical lions thought to have died out in Africa decades ago. They have long, wide, black manes which reach under their bellies. The male cats, descendants of lions kept at the royal palace by Emperor Haile Selassie, have the physical features of the North African Barbary lion or South Africa's Cape lion; the two subspecies probably developed similar features because cool winters and the lack of dense bush allowed their manes to grow longer.

❧ German scientists have rediscovered a dwarf maki [lemur] weighing just over an ounce. This nocturnal and mouse-sized creature, the world's smallest primate, was first described in 1852, but then forgotten. Only about a dozen have ever been seen.

Robson wrote to describe how she saw a pigeon board "the tube" and travel one stop from Paddington. "With their renowned navigational abilities, is it possible the pigeon knew where it was going?" she asked.

Other Brits shared her amazement. Jim Brock regularly saw a light-reddish pigeon travel one stop from Paddington during the mid-1970s. More recently, Sabiha Foster noted a 1994 sighting: "A pair of pigeons hopped onto the Circle Line at Aldgate, stayed by the door and alighted with purpose at the next stop, Tower Hill. How did they know that the platform for Tower Hill was the same side of the carriage as that for Aldgate?" Eric Simms also suggested higher avian intelligence in *The Street Life of the London Pigeon;* in this volume, Simms recorded observing a pigeon that boarded his Kilburn train and trav-

eled two stops—where it joined three other pigeons on the platform.

Chris Harbard, a spokesman for the Royal Society for the Protection of Birds, was skeptical. "A pigeon's only incentive to hop on a train is to look for food," he asserted. This contradicts the observation of Lorna Read, who saw a pigeon hop into a Northern Line carriage at King's Cross. Tourists then "tried to tempt it with potato chips, but, unusually, the bird wasn't interested. . . . As soon as the doors opened at Euston it flew out. . . . I feel quite sure that travel, not food, was the purpose," she wrote.

CASSOCK COMMOTION

A vicar continued praying when a ferret disappeared up his cassock during a

SCHWASCAR

THE SCHWASCAR AWARDS

DOGGED JOURNEYS

❤ In January, a four-year-old dog called Deni was reunited with his master, a young Croatian Serb called Goran Radanovic, in Ruma refugee camp, 50 miles north of Belgrade. Radanovic had earlier fled from Petrinja, 30 miles southeast of Zagreb. Deni had braved the bitter Balkan winter, walking more than 300 miles in four and a half months to find his master, in a place the dog had never seen.

RUNNERS-UP

❤ In March, another dog found its Serb refugee owners after a seven-month, 380-mile odyssey.

❤ A golden retriever called Coconut Harry disappeared from the boat of his owner, Naomi Simonelli, during rough weather off the Florida Keys on April 14. The coast guard could find no trace of the 80-pound dog; but eight days later he turned up, shaggier and 15 pounds lighter, on tiny Key Lois— known as "Monkey Island" because its only inhabitants are the hundreds of monkeys raised for sale to research laboratories. He had braved strong currents as he swam about five miles.

❤ Last March, a border collie called Alfie was left outside a shop in Plymouth, England, while his owner, Laura Knight, browsed inside. The dog took a bus home to Plympton. He tried to get off at the stop for the Lynham Inn, where Laura's father is the landlord, but the bus driver barred the way because he thought Alfie might hurt himself. He was turned over at a police station, where he was collected later by Laura. "Dad thought Alfie was fretting about being late for his job guarding the pub so he hopped on the number 21 to get home on time for opening," she said.

communion service. The Rev. Stephen Grey, of St. Michael's Church, Barnford, near Rochdale, Greater Manchester, was alerted to the interloper when a woman worshiper screamed and jumped up on a pew.

"I looked up and there it was, staring at me," he said. "It went three times around my cassock and then stuck its head underneath." Eventually, the ferret, believed to be a pet, was ejected from the church after biting a parishioner's thumb. "I was trained to carry on regardless, but I must admit the prayers speeded up a bit towards the end," said Mr. Grey.

TURTLE TRAVELS

A loggerhead turtle called Rosita released in California in July 1994 turned up last November in Japan, 6,500 miles away, farther than any other sea creature has been known to swim. It is now believed that loggerheads are born in Japan, migrate to California as hatchlings and swim back at the age of 30 to nest, a round trip of 13,000 miles.

SMUGGLE UP

•A Russian arrested at Cairo airport was smuggling two crocodiles, two foxes, five jerboas, twelve snakes, seventeen chameleons and twenty-eight lizards in his luggage.

•A woman who tried to smuggle 75 live snakes in her bra was picked up and arrested by Swedish customs officers in Stockholm on May 13. They had seen her scratching at her chest in a suspicious way.

I THINK I'VE GOT A BITE

There is a new hazard for watersports enthusiasts at the Lac de la Ganguise, a French holiday resort: piranha. Two of these predatory fish, usually residents of South America, were reeled in by astonished fishermen. One, measuring 14 inches from stem to stern, put up quite a struggle. The other, caught by Jean-Marc Simon, measured over 18 inches. Spotting it near the surface, he quickly baited his hook. "Five minutes later I brought up this thing."

The "thing" caused a stir among the gendarmes and fish experts before it was handed over to the Natural History Museum in Paris for identification. Although a local official declared the lake safe for bathers, saying that piranhas were dangerous only in shoals, the few brave swimmers were outnumbered by anglers after the catch of a lifetime.

This is not the first time piranha have been found in French waters.

Two were caught by anglers in the Garonne River in 1991. They are a popular pet and are readily available for between 50 and 100 francs. The explanation that they were dumped by a bored aquarium keeper or prankster is highly plausible. We wonder how many more piranha are still out there.

OTTER SPLATTER

An otter run over by a naturalist in Nottinghamshire, England, was the first to be spotted in the country for 40 years. The body of the otter, an adult male, was given to a museum which prepared it for display.

P. O.'D

Sweden is exporting synthetic wolf urine to Kuwait, where it is sprayed on roads to prevent camels from colliding with cars. During the 1994 Olympic Games in Lillehammer, Norway, the method was used to stop elks from straying onto mountain roads.

BOARISH BEHAVIOR

Wild boars have returned to Hampshire, England's New Forest after an absence of 90 years. In late March, the great-grandson of Charlie Bessant, a gamekeeper who shot the forest's last wild boar in 1905, led 13 of the animals into an eight-acre sanctuary.

Peter Bessant, a Forestry Commission worker, said wild boars were once considered pests by farmers. "Old Charlie was just doing his job," he said. "If he knew his great-grandson would one day greet the boar's return, I'm sure he would have approved."

ATTACKS BY ANIMALS

LOVER BULLS

A police car taking a drunkard to a lockup in Kolsva, Sweden, was suddenly surrounded by 20 lovesick bulls who had escaped from a nearby farm. One bull mounted the hood, while others rubbed against the doors or caressed the trunk. "Under the circumstances, we did not find it urgent to leave our car until the rutting horde was distracted by a lorry," said one constable. Farm workers finally managed to lead the runaways back to their field.

PET FOOD

Frans Heemskerk, 69, a retired hatter and reclusive cat lover in Leiden, Holland, was "almost totally eaten" by his 20 pets after he died, leaving them without food. The body was not found for three weeks. Ten cats were caught and put down, but a number fled.

GOOSED

Dutchman Anne Osinga, 60, chairman of the Frisian Society for the Protection of Birds, had his cheek bone broken after being knocked down by a dead goose. The six-pound bird fell 75 feet after being shot by one of Osinga's hunting companions on December 15.

REALLY MAD COW DISEASE

In late May, Bob Floyd, 66, of Chipping Norton, England, was found with his ear torn off and blood pouring from his head in a field surrounded by a herd of cows. He and his family had been antique shopping when he decided to take his dog for a walk. Half an hour later, the dog returned alone. Floyd, who had suffered a brain tumor three years earlier, was later released from the hospital.

SNAKE BITTEN

Valentin Grimaldo, 40, was out walking with his brother along U.S. 281 near Encino, Texas, when he was bitten on the hand by a poisonous coral snake. He bit its head off, skinned it and used the skin as a tourniquet to keep the venom from spreading. A passerby drove him to a hospital and he was expected to recover.

KNOCK YOUR SPOTS OFF

South African oil worker Erik van Heerden, 37, was attacked by a leopard in Botswana. Punching the animal didn't work, so he grabbed its throat and strangled it. He suffered only minor scratches and bites.

HELD HOSTAGE BY ROOK RAGE

At 4 a.m. on June 9, three-year-old Charlotte Dunnatt was disturbed by a tapping noise on her window. Pulling back the curtains to investigate, she was confronted by a yellow-eyed feathered fiend flapping against the frame and pecking at the double glazing. For the next two days, rooks hurled themselves against the windows of the Chichester, England, home.

The converted barn is named Owl House, but no owls or other birds had caused any problems since the family moved in a year ago. However, Charlotte's mother Rosemarie said: "This is not the first time we have been attacked by birds. At our other house we had some problems with magpies." During the latest attack, Mr. Dunnatt attached pieces of string and paper to the windows and hung models of other birds from the frames, but noth-

ANIMAL ANOMALIES

David Dougal keeps a tight hold on his racing pigeon, having already had two fly off to Morocco.

❦ Maurice, a cat in Wellington, New Zealand, has been caught stealing women's underwear. On nocturnal forays, he showed a penchant for undershirts and bras, amassing about 60 items. Fiona, his owner, washed and folded them all, but no one has come forward to claim any.

❦ Two racing pigeons from England have settled in Casablanca, independently, four months apart. The first, a female Bushart cross, was supposed to have raced from Beau Vois, France, to David Dougal's home in Humshaugh, England, last June. Instead, she headed southwest to the North African coast, settling in the loft owned by Essofi Mohamed. In October 1995, the second bird, a nephew of the first, set off from his owner's allotment, flying the 1,500 miles to join his aunt. "I couldn't believe it when I got another letter from Essofi," said Mr. Dougal. "When the first bird went missing we weren't really too surprised because it was awful weather for the race and that affects the bird's homing instincts. But there is no explanation we can come up with for the nephew. He was only a few weeks old and had just learned to fly."

❦ Early last October, Pia Bischoff found a strange kitten near a hay loft in Dybvad, Denmark. Its fur and even its claws are green, and the color doesn't wash off. A vet said that the cat was perfectly healthy despite a copper patina, apparently present since birth, from the tip of its fur to the hair follicles. Some years ago, the hair of several blond women in southern Sweden turned green—a phenomenon eventually traced to water from corroded copper pipes. Pia is now waiting for the results of blood tests at the State Hospital in Copenhagen to see if the cat has any copper in its blood.

CATS UNDERFOOT

❧ In a house under renovation only two doors from his Teignmouth, England home, a four-year-old cat called Bruno was trapped beneath the floorboards for 45 days—and survived. Bruno had probably crawled under the floorboards, which were soon nailed back into place; when his faint cries finally led builder Derek Snell to the rescue, the cat was 6 pounds lighter than his pre-disappearance weight of 14. "The poor thing was like a sack of bones with a head," recalls Aubrey Pitts, the pet's owner. "He suffered temporary blindness through the shock and the vet initally thought he'd had a stroke. He must have eaten spiders; there are no mice on that floor and it was dry as a bone. I cannot believe he lasted that long without any water." Bruno returned to health after several days on an IV.

❧ Another cat, nine-year-old Tog, survived being walled up for two months in a Scotland house. Tog went missing in February from the Eardley family's farm near Insch. She was found, alive but emaciated, after another couple moved in to a partly converted steading opposite and became aware of strange noises behind a wall.

ing worked. A local farmer has suggested they capture a rook with a rat trap and hang its body upside down for the other birds to see.

A spokesman for the Royal Society for Prevention of Cruelty to Animals said the phenomenon was unusual, but not paranormal; it is often caused by rooks mistaking their reflection for other rooks which they try to drive away.

FISH STORY

Bob Ringewold and his friend Verna Dawn were driving near Lake Michigan in a rental car when they spotted a young eagle flying overhead with a wriggling fish in its talons. "And then," Mr. Ringewold recalled, "kabam!" The fish slammed into the car roof, leaving a large dent. Ringewold retrieved the five-and-a-half-pound fish, a sucker, to serve as evidence for Avis Rent-A-Car.

TRAPPER JOHN

Attempting to leave her bathroom, 70-year-old Ginette Turner-Dupuis found herself trapped when her cats knocked open a cupboard door that wedged against the exit. After six hours, the senior resorted to breaking a window and calling for help.

FATAL ERROR

After the shredded remains of a Florida diver's scuba suit were found, George Burgess, keeper of the International Shark Attack File, said, "We prefer to call most of these incidents 'interactions' rather than attacks because they are cases of mistaken identity when a shark is going after a meal."

FEEDING TIME

For the second time in nine months, the big cats at Guatemala's national zoo helped an unhappy man meet his maker. On June 18, Mario Leonardo Quan Mata, 35, scaled two high fences before hurling himself into a cage containing two adult tigers. Last August, a gun shop owner was killed by jaguars at the zoo after jumping into their cage.

PYTHON TRIES
TO SWALLOW MAN

A giant python was caught trying to swallow a rubber tapper near Tenang in Malaysia's Johor State at 10:30 p.m. on September 4. It had already squeezed him to death, as was later shown by his multiple fractures in the neck, rib and cervical regions. Star-tled by flashlights, the reptile released the bloody head of Ee Heng Chuan, 29, with a violent shake.

Naturalist Dr. Khew Bong Heang said it was common for pythons to devour chickens and goats, but attacks on humans were rarer. Although a human head could easily be swallowed, he said, "the snake might not be able to expand its jaws to accommodate the width of the human shoulders."

The python, 21 feet, 10 inches long, with a diameter of 30 inches and weighing about 63 pounds, was thought to be the largest ever caught in the country. It was estimated to be about 40 years old.

GO WILD!

❂ Josh Carlisle, a ten-year-old with Down's syndrome, was playing in his yard in Cassville, Missouri, when a couple of stray dogs apparently caught his eye and he followed them into the rugged, wooded Ozarks near his home. For three days, in below-freezing temperatures, up to 350 volunteers searched for the boy. On March 9, Oscar "Junior" Nell, on horseback, heard barking and found Josh with the two protective dogs in a creek bed about one and a half miles from his house. "The dogs took him in as if they were his mother," said Sheriff Ralph Hendrix, somewhat ungrammatically. "They probably curled up next to him and kept him warm, warm enough to stay alive on us." Josh's mother and stepfather planned to give the strays a new home.

❂ Student Liz Hutton was staying in a sports club hut west of Auckland, New Zealand, when, on the evening of June 4, 1993, she took a walk, wearing pajamas, oilskin and shoes. She was lost in the bush for three very wet and cold nights. Hundreds of people joined the search. Just as she was being given up for dead, her father and three helpers found her huddled under a tree, cold, wet and hungry, but uninjured. Her life had been saved by Eva, her six-year-old (and very fat) pet Labrador, which slept on top of her during the nights.

❂ Amos Johnson, a 79-year-old farmer from Easingwold, England, slipped into a ditch while freeing a lamb from a hawthorn bush, and was trapped by the bush for 16 hours. His life was saved by Bess, his nine-year-old Border collie, who snuggled against him and kept him warm until he was discovered by his brother who heard Bess barking.

POODLE SNATCHERS TAKE FLIGHT

❣ A spate of attempted poodle-nappings in northern Maine began in Greenville on January 5, 1995, when a 20-pound poodle-Pekingese cross-bred dog was carried away and killed by a large great horned owl. Game wardens tracked down the errant bird, which "barely weighed three pounds," and shot it later that day. We move quickly on from the mystery of whether a three-pound bird can snatch a 20-pound dog (which is presumably resisting) to the greater mystery of dognapping birds. Within the week, Robyn Kinney of East Corinth saw her white poodle being attacked by an owl with a four-foot wingspan. The 15-pound pet would have been carried away if it had not escaped to hide in a car. This bird stayed to swoop on human pedestrians, but flew away before it could be shot.

That would have been that, had we not found a tiny note in July that simply said that a large owl had been shot by wardens in Maine as it flew off with its eleventh poodle. Tragically, its last victim also perished as the blasted owl fell to the ground.

BATTY

Starving vampire bats attacked more than 40 peasants during March in the village of El Pozon, 69 miles east of the Salvadorian capital of San Salvador. The bats usually feed on birds and other animals, mainly cows.

TERRORS OF THE DEEP

A six-foot conger eel nearly killed a diving instructor while he was giving a lesson in Loch Long, Scotland. Gordon Bell, 32, was teaching three pupils how to dive at night on August 30 when he was attacked.

The creature was disturbed by the beam from his flashlight as he swam into an area 90 feet below the surface nicknamed "Conger Alley" because of its large eel population.

Mr. Bell's neck became entangled in a length of fishing line which had been half swallowed by the eel. He was dragged down 60 feet further at high speed into a deep trench. In cutting himself free, he severed his oxygen line by mistake.

He swam as quickly as he could to the surface and, although suffering from the bends, managed to cross the loch and drag himself out of the water.

Mr. Bell was found by a passing cyclist nine hours later, lying unconscious on a roadside shoulder more than two miles from the spot he was last seen.

He recovered at home in Glasgow after four hours in a decompression chamber at Faslane Naval Base.

HARD BITTEN

A boy of nine died six hours after being bitten by a rabid dog in Bucharest. He was the second child to have died of rabies this year in Romania, where thousands of stray dogs roam the capital. The cases are thought to be the first rabies deaths in Europe for more than a decade.

48

ATTACKS ON ANIMALS

LOVED TO DEATH

The killer of 200 female sea lions turned out to be a giant bull sea lion with a crush on the ladies. Every year the carcasses of about 40 females have littered a cove near San Miguel Island off the Californian coast. At first, fisherman were suspected of shooting them; but a National Marine Fisheries biologist, Robert DeLong, spotted a massive bull sea lion mating with a female. She was gasping and died within a minute.

The bull is a cross between a California and a Stellar sea lion, and he seems confused about everything from the time to breed to the way to go about it. Male California sea lions usually weigh about 900 pounds, but the hybrid weighs around 1,600 pounds, eight times the weight of an average female.

MURDER MOST FOWL

Roderick Baker, a 50-year-old antiques dealer, tried to ward off police by holding 140 chickens hostage at knifepoint. The trouble began on June 27 when sanitation workers were sent to clean up Baker's trash-filled yard in Uniondale, New York. Baker produced a large knife and threatened to kill one chicken a minute if the authorities didn't get off his property. He carried out his threat, beheading three birds before the police moved in and arrested him. He was charged with obstruction of governmental administration and two violations of agriculture and market laws before being released.

The surviving chickens were moved to a farm on Long Island to "live a normal chicken life," according to Larry Wallach of the ASPCA.

SNAKE HARMER

A woman in Jamestown, New York, accused of ripping her boyfriend's python in half during an argument, was charged with torturing animals and criminal mischief. Laurie Riley, 22, was at the apartment of her boyfriend, Bruce Miller, 25, on January 22, when she took the three-foot-long Burmese python from its tank, placed it over her knee and pulled in opposite directions, killing it.

DIAL-A-FISH NETS CATCH IN BORNEO

In the past year, about 900 of the 3,500 Telekom Malaysia pay phones have been stolen in Sabah, Borneo. It was discovered that fishermen cut off the handsets and lowered them into the water after connecting them to

PECULIAR PRESS

KNIFE-WIELDING MONKEY GOES BANANAS IN PENNSYLVANIA
Attleboro (Mass.) Sun-Chronicle,
March 3, 1995

IRISH PEAT BOGS ROCKED BY GREAT SHEEP EXPLOSION
Independent, July 13, 1995

MICE TO BE BOMBED
Today, August 15, 1995

high-powered batteries. The electricity passing through the microphones produced a high-pitched sound that attracted fish into the nets. "If we were manufacturers of fishing tackle, we'd be delighted," said Telekom spokesman Ahmad Zaini Mohammad Amin. "Unfortunately, we're a phone company, so it's a bit of a disaster." General Shahrom Abdul Majid, head of the local fisheries department, pointed out that fishermen on the east coast of Malaysia knock bamboo sticks underwater to produce a sound which attracts a particular species of fish, while some aquarists in Japan pipe music into tanks and the fish move to the rhythm, almost as if they were dancing.

WILD AT HEART

Lumberjack Peter King, 37, who caught rabies after having sex with a raccoon, denied animal cruelty charges in Jasper, Tennessee. He claimed the raccoon was already dead.

MOO-TILATION

A mutilated cow was discovered near Camlough, England, last September. The carcass had been drained of blood, the flesh stripped from the skull and the vital organs removed. Investigators suggested that the damage was caused by animal predators, but Miles Johnson, an electronic technician and

ANIMAL VS. ANIMAL

A bird in the paw is worth two in the bush; this cat wound up with neither, despite a six-foot leap.

❦ Leaping two yards into the air to attack a sea eagle at the Okayama Nature Reserve in Japan, this kamikaze kitty narrowly missed sinking its claws into the seven-foot wingspan bird of prey. Considering the eagle's razor-sharp talons and flesh-ripping beak, perhaps it's just as well.

❦ Israeli belly dancer "Lillian" of Eilat gave her nine-foot Burmese python a rat for lunch, but the rat took so many bites out of the snake that she had to fly it to Rambam Hospital in Haifa, where a vet said the bites had injured its spinal cord. "The reptile will survive," he said, "but his slithering days are over."

❦ A South African puppy called Licky was carried off from its owner's back yard by a crowned eagle which flew off towards a tree. Licky wriggled free and fell 15 feet headfirst into a suburban swimming pool. Licky was rushed to a clinic where she was treated for concussion, water in the lungs and talon punctures on the neck.

ufologist, maintained that "the organs were sucked out through a clean incision made by some high-tech laser device." In keeping with the classic "mute" scenario in 1970s America, witnesses had told of a large, black, silent helicopter and various UFOs in the area at the time of the mutilation. These included discs and a ball of light with a smaller ball revolving around it.

MAN BITES DOG

Arnim John Kudinow of Lake Oswego, Oregon, has been sentenced to 18 months in prison for ramming a police car with his pickup truck, throwing a knife at officers and biting a police dog on the nose as it tried to catch him by biting his arm. The dog, a Dutch Malinois named Ronnie, died from a streptococcus infection three weeks later. Police said the bite was to blame. Kudinow bit the dog after a 17-mile chase last December, when a gas station attendant reported the driver appeared drunk.

"DEMON" CROCODILES BURN TO DEATH

A male and female crocodile, captured on the outskirts of Cameroon's capital, were burned alive in public by traditional healers who said the three-foot-long animals were bewitched.

Up to 300 residents of Yaounde's Madagascar and Nkomkana districts watched on September 24 as the healers adorned the male reptile with a beard and pants, and the female with hair and red nail polish on its claws, before setting them ablaze on a wooden funeral pyre. Locals, who chipped in for the cost of the gasoline, blamed the male for a spate of road accidents on a bridge under which it lived, and some believed that both of the beasts were responsible for the disappearance of small children. Sightings of crocodiles are rare in Yaounde, a city of nearly one million people.

That, at any rate, was how Reuters reported the tale; however, readers of the *Ethiopian Herald,* quoting the official Cameroon News Agency (CAMNEWS), were told there was only one croc, 98 inches long, captured by five witch doctors in a pool at Nlongkak on the outskirts of Yaounde. Moreover, the animal was already sporting trousers, with snout and claws painted red.

The witch doctors said its male companion had escaped, but would be captured soon. They asserted that the reptile was a transformed old woman who had also appeared as a python and had caused the death of many people, especially children, through accidents. After incantations and rituals, the hapless croc was burned.

MONKEY BUSINESS

On December 12, a schoolteacher in the Calcutta suburb of Domjur shot a monkey that entered his garden. The primate hobbled to the adjacent police compound and lay there writhing. Local people took the animal to a veterinary clinic but it died. When the body was brought back to the police station, more than 50 monkeys from the neighborhood gathered, shrieked loudly and refused to leave for hours. A local Communist Party politician, apparently moved by the monkey's protest, filed a complaint with the police asking them to arrest the schoolteacher who had shot the monkey. Police did not take any action.

SCHWASCAR

THE SCHWASCAR AWARDS

ANIMAL CRACKERS

❤ Pam Mansfield shares her two-bedroom, semidetached house in Etton, England, with a staggering 166 pets, including 25 monkeys, nine pythons, three iguanas and an alligator. Her husband and 14-year-old son manage to squeeze in somewhere. Pam, 45, started her zoo some twenty years ago when she took in an injured falcon. She recently turned down the offer of a shark and three Himalayan sun bears for lack of space, but in August she was about to take in an emu, a gibbon and two Shetland ponies.

❤ Some animal collectors specialize in one species. Jack and Donna Wright, of Kingston, Ontario, for instance, have the world's largest collection of cats—689 of them, last we heard. Donna rises at 5:30 a.m. to start emptying, cleaning and refilling ten large cat litter trays. She goes through 154 pounds of litter a day, emptying the trays four times. The feline horde requires a daily supply of 180 large cans of meat, 55 pounds of dry cat food, $10\frac{1}{2}$ pints of milk and countless bowls of water.

Each cat has been named and the Wrights make a point of distinguishing one cat from another. It all began with Midnight, a long-haired black cat owned by Donna when she married Jack in 1970. Then Midnight had kittens, stray cats were brought to the Wrights and things steadily got out of hand. Donna, 52, owns a painting company and Jack, 55, is a painter, but the cats' care takes everything they own and then some.

At night, 30 or more cats settle on their bed, the combined weight pressing down like so many sandbags and making a change of position difficult for the humans. Then there's the problem of eating with so many cats around: "I'll tell you what's hard to eat in here," says Donna. "Kentucky Fried Chicken. Every time I eat it I have to walk around the house with the plate under my chin."

❤ Another large Canadian cat colony was dispersed in February 1993 when a woman of 83 fainted from dehydration and malnutrition in her small house near Lockport, north of Winnipeg. After the daughter ran to a neighbor's house for help, welfare workers discovered about 100 cats.

There was electricity in the women's house, but no running water; the two melted snow for drinking and washing. A bucket served as a bathroom, and the walls were black with mildew. Kittens were found nestling inside a sofa, a mattress and holes in the wall. The women, who spent nearly all their money on cat food, subsisted on tea and dry toast; their house was ruled unfit for human habitation.

❤ John Bellamy, an unemployed man in his thirties, was briefly arrested last March when he tried to prevent access to his pet rats. Bellamy reared them in cages piled up to the ceilings in every room of his bungalow in Ditton Fields, England. He had been interbreeding domestic rats with wild varieties, producing huge hybrids. Some were 18 inches long and quite plump. Though health inspectors took away about 150 in cages and spent three days killing more than 80 that were loose, even more may have escaped. Rat droppings reached the window in the living room; there were dead rats everywhere, including the freezer and microwave; and the stench was overpowering.

SWARMINGS

INSECTOVISION

Hundreds of television viewers on the Scottish island of Iona lost their picture after a swarm of earwigs broke into the island's transmitter box and ate some of the components.

SNAILS ON THE RAILS

A horde of snails swarmed onto the rails of the Casablanca-Fez line in Morocco, bringing an express train to a slippery halt near Meknes, 87 miles north of Rabat. The track was blocked for several hours. Heavy rain had coaxed the snails from under cover and, mysteriously, they often congregated at that spot on the railway line.

FROG MARCH

A column of migrating toads over 1,000 miles long snaked through China's Liaoning Province. Residents in Benxi City watched in awe as the toads traveled along the Taize River. Most were newly born and no longer than a fingernail, while larger ones were said to be spaced out every 30 feet, leading the others along.

WHAT A BUZZ

A beekeeper called in to investigate a low buzzing sound found 10,000 bees in five colonies beneath the Darlington, England, home of reporter Beezy Marsh. They could not be removed in safety and had to be exterminated.

GO WILD!

❧ Last June, Zejna Elkaz, 46, was discovered living in the wilds of the central Bosnian highlands. She had last been seen on November 2, 1992, when Chetniks (Bosnian Serb militiamen) laid waste to the village of Cvitovici where she lived. They crowded 11 villagers—Muslims and Croats—into a house and threw a grenade through the open door, killing Ms. Elkaz's mother and six others. Ms. Elkaz escaped by jumping out of a window.

After four bitter winters with temperatures sometimes plunging to -4°F, she had been given up for dead. However, she survived for 44 months in a shelter made from branches and plastic sheeting, on a diet of mushrooms, walnuts and berries.

The wolves and bears never attacked her. "Some of the bears were huge—440 pounds, at least—and there were times when they came within one and a half meters of me. But I would bang on a piece of plastic and they would run away. I was never scared of them. We learned to live with one another. The bears would climb up the trees and break off a branch, and then sit on the ground eating the fruit. But they always left some fruit behind and I think that was for me."

The doctor who examined her, Enes Ribic, a fellow Muslim returnee, said: "She is a biological phenomenon. I have looked at the books and found no record of any woman living wild for that length of time."

THE SCHWASCAR AWARDS

HEROIC ANIMAL

❣ In the central Chinese town of Beiling, Li-Shuhua and his family were awoken by their three-year-old cat named Ugly Sister on July 16, 1995. The cat meowed and scratched at their legs and then jumped on a windowsill and pushed open the window. When the family of six didn't follow her, Ugly Sister jumped down and started pulling at the trousers of her owner. Li then noticed that mud was starting to fall from the wall of the two-story mud house and, seconds after he rushed his family outside, the whole building collapsed.

RUNNERS-UP

❣ A stray dog urinated on a Semtex bomb in a doorway in the Czech town of Domazlice and saved the lives of five people. The pee-soaked hammer kept the bomb from exploding.

❣ In 1942, Sergeant Cyril Jones (now 81) parachuted into Sumatra in an attempt to hold up the Japanese advance across Southeast Asia. His parachute got snagged in the branches of a tree and for 12 days he hung there unable to cut himself down. Mr. Jones would certainly have died had it not been for a monkey that befriended him and brought him food. "We became very close friends and the monkey started bringing me bananas," he said. "Sometimes he would bring me bamboo shoots, which he showed me how to eat." He finally managed to cut himself down, but the monkey followed him, bringing him fruit until Mr. Jones was caught by Japanese soldiers. The monkey followed him to the prison camp. "I had to get rid of him because he turned on the Japanese soldiers when they tried to bully me," he recalled.

❣ Nelson, a one-eyed parrot, kept calling out "Mum, mum, hello!" until his owner's family discovered the house was on fire. The humans fled the house in Bournemouth, England, but, unfortunately Nelson died in the blaze along with a hamster, a footless macaw and two finches.

❣ A group of diving trainees sailing in the Red Sea near the Egyptian resort of Sharm el-Sheikh on July 23 saw some dolphins and jumped into the sea to join them. Martin Richardson, 29, was the last to head back to the boat. Suddenly, he felt a shark biting his thigh. "It let go of me and swam out and then came back and bit my front. I punched it with my right hand. It swam away again and came back and got me above the right nipple and took a hunk of flesh out. My friends pulled me out of the water. They said it was the dolphins that saved me." Tony Heap, one of Richardson's human rescuers, gives absolute credit: "The dolphins scared the shark off. They were swimming into the shark. There must have been five or six of them." Mr. Richardson underwent surgery overnight, made a good recovery and was able to walk by the following afternoon; doctors said he might have been attacked by two sharks after they found different-sized bite marks on his body.

NEW SPECIES FOUND

IT'S A NEW MAMMAL

Panay cloudrunner's future is a race against the chainsaw.

An unknown mammal species, a nocturnal, squirrel-like rodent, has been discovered on the island of Panay in the central Philippines. Called the Panay cloudrunner, or *Crateromys heaneyi*, it was found as scientists race the chainsaw in the island's rapidly shrinking forests. It's a tree-climber, weighs more than two pounds, has a tail longer than its body and, according to local hunters, rarely leaves its den during the day. Its vocalizations include a shrill, almost insect-like cry. "The cloudrunner is very similar in size, appearance and habits to our North American fox squirrel," said Robert Kennedy, a researcher at the Cincinnati Museum of Natural History and Science, "but the fox squirrel is diurnal, eats nuts instead of fruit and it has a somewhat bushier tail." Three cloudrunners, two males and a female, are on display in the Cincinnati Zoo.

LIFE, BUT CERTAINLY NOT AS WE KNOW IT

Tiny creatures found clinging to the mouths of lobsters have been awarded the ultimate taxonomic accolade—a phylum all to themselves. The new phylum, the Cycliophora, is only the 36th ever described for all 30–100 million species. The single species so far discovered, *Symbion pandora*, behaves like an animated cold sore. The name Cycliophora is Greek for "carrying a small wheel." This is because the creature has a circular feeding tunnel coated with fine fronds, located right next to its anus.

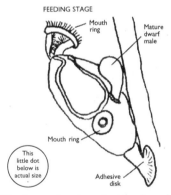

FEEDING STAGE
Mouth ring
Mature dwarf male
Mouth ring
This little dot below is actual size
Adhesive disk

The larva develops inside the adult by a process of asexual budding, which makes it a genetic clone of its parent. Periodically, the parent sheds its upper half which includes the nervous system as well as a disintegrating mouth and gut, and like the objects that flew out of Pandora's box, the larva escapes. Meanwhile, the adult's lost organs are replaced by new ones that began forming inside it well before they were needed.

Symbion pandora has an alternative sexual reproductive cycle in which a

SERPENTINE TALES

❦ On August 9, 1994, a man lifted the toilet seat in his Staffanstorp, Sweden, home to be faced with the head and upper part of an eight-foot boa constrictor. The boa was a house pet that had been left in a neighboring apartment's bathroom six days earlier to cool off during a heatwave. The snake retreated, and panic soon spread. An unfounded rumor circulated that the fugitive boa was pregnant and had been hiding to give birth—and thereby infest the sewers. After many hours of pumping, poking around with rubber tubes and surveillance with miniature TV cameras, the public enemy was flushed out.

❦ Singapore's former discus and shot-put champion, Fok Keng Choy, was in a Malaysian restroom sometime in August 1993 when he was bitten on the testicles by a python.

❦ Singapore snakes struck again in February 1995 when condominium residents were terrified after eight sightings in toilet bowls. Descriptions of the intruder varied from "grey with white spots" to "brown with stripes." Realizing a good offense is the best defense, Francis Lim, assistant curator at the Singapore Zoo, suggested flushing toilets before use, as the commotion would scare any snake. He also suggested pouring bleach down the toilets to create an irritating environment that snakes would shun.

❦ Elizabeth Roak was annoyed that her two cats were gone when she returned from vacation on September 15, 1995. She found broken glass and fallen shelves in the basement of her house in Whitemarsh, Pennsylvania. However, fright commandeered all her emotions when she opened a door to her cellar and saw a 13-foot diamondback rattlesnake crawling towards her. She only saw about one-third of it and didn't know how huge it was until after it had been shot by the police. It was about seven inches in diameter and had a yellow underbelly. Police thought it could have been an escaped pet and "might have been a python." Roak thought the snake got into her basement to drink from the cats' bowl. The cats subsequently returned.

❦ Roak's serpent was dwarfed by the one that slithered into a Colorado Springs bedroom on June 20, 1994. Lisa Billingsley was woken by a hiss and told her companion Eddie Donald that there was something on the floor. He turned on the light and saw an 18-foot snake. The snake, a boa constrictor about 18 inches in circumference, had pushed back the window screen and slid inside. It took six policemen and a Humane Society officer to carry the 120-pound creature out of the house. Its provenance was unknown.

dwarf, nonfeeding male, possibly with two penises, lives attached to the female; waiting for her to release a miniature female without a brain but bearing a single ovum, which he fertilizes. Before releasing her clone, the host female dissolves from the inside, becoming a sort of soup held together by a bag of skin.

Asexual adults are bottle-shaped and 347 micrometers (about one-third of a millimeter) long. These bizarre creatures are described in the December 1995 *Nature* by Peter Funch and Reinhardt Mobjerg Kristensen, invertebrate zoologists at the University of Copenhagen.

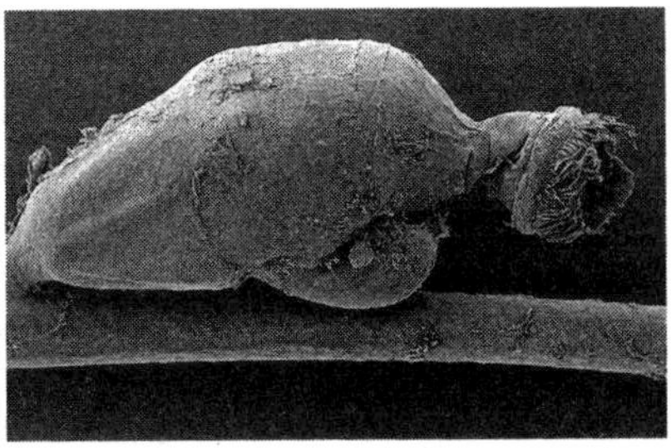

Symbion pandora *is a completely new type of creature.*

It was, in fact, Kristensen who described the last new phylum, the Locifera, discovered in Roscoff, France, in 1983. These tiny creatures live between sand grains and have a retractable head and thorax.

KEEPING AN EYE ON THE SIGNS OF THE THAI

A female elephant sprouting black tusks has been found in Thailand's northern Phayao Province. It is extremely rare for female elephants to develop tusks, and even then they are almost invariably white. Veterinarians said that the three-inch tusks sported by Noi, an elephant belonging to Kamnu Boadaeng, were authentically black and might grow a bit longer.

TWO-TOISE

The first known Siamese twin tortoises (as opposed to two-headers) were born in late July at Israel's Hebrew University. They might survive but share too many organs to be separated.

MASS DEATHS

ALL WASHED UP

More than 4,700 dead snakes, many of them poisonous, washed ashore in southwestern Japan during the first week of 1996, stuffed in unmarked wooden crates. It was suggested that they had fallen off a cargo ship near Jeju Do Island in South Korea. The discovery of about 90 such boxes was confirmed in Yamaguchi, Fukuoka and Nagasaki prefectures.

Most of the snakes were identified as vipers found mainly in the Yangtze River basin in China. Six were identified as "Akamadara mamushi" *(Dinodon rufozonatus)* or "Tairiku mamushi" *(Agkistrodon brevicauds)*, both of which are found in China and on the Korean Peninsula, where they are often eaten as a tonic. On January 6 alone, Nagasaki police received reports of 1,350 snakes in 28 wooden boxes and a bag containing another 30 snakes washing up in nine spots in Kyushu. About 60 similar boxes containing 3,700 dead snakes had already been found on the northern shores of Kyushu and the nearby small island of Tsushima since the morning of January 2.

Some experts suggested that the snakes might have been destined for use in Chinese medicine, for pickling in alcoholic drinks, or for the restaurant business. Alcohol with snake extract is widely believed to boost energy levels and sells at high prices.

MANIMALS

SPRING-HEELED JACK IN INDIA

Creatures that walk like dogs, have faces like pigs, eyes like bulbs and springs on their feet were sighted driving a white van through the central and eastern parts of Uttar Pradesh, northern India, in search of small children to eat, according to a report in the *Pioneer* newspaper on June 25.

"The manai [man] walks both like a man and an animal. His eyes and shoes have bulbs, his shoes have springs and he jumps 80 feet at one go," a man from Patti village was quoted as saying. "There are many like him. They come in groups in a white Maruti van, which can fly over any obstruction on the road."

Villagers say that at least 20 children have already fallen prey to the seemingly unstoppable beasts. Manju, an eight-year-old girl who says she saw one of the creatures, described a man with the face of a pig who walked on all fours. A village woman said that the man first walked on four legs, but subsequently took flight.

PECULIAR PRESS

HAIRDO KILLS MUM
Daily Mirror, October 7, 1994

DOGS ARE BEING TAUGHT TO DO HOUSEWORK FOR THE DISABLED
Evening Herald (Dublin), October 21, 1995

ECUADOR'S PRESIDENT DECLARES HE'S NOT DEAD
Record (Hackensack, New Jersey), September 27, 1994

DWARF BATMAN TERRORIZES ZANZIBAR

Last year, there was widespread fear in Zanzibar concerning the return of the *popobawa,* a dwarf with a Cyclops eye, small pointed ears, bat wings and talons, notorious for swooping into houses and raping men. The name is derived from the Swahili words for "bat" and "wing."

One victim was Mjaka Hamad, a soft-spoken peasant farmer aged 55 from the village of Sogea. At first he thought it was a dream, but the stifling force pushing him into his mattress dragged him from his sleep. "I couldn't imagine what was happening to me," he said. "You feel as if you are screaming with no voice. It was just like a dream, but then I was thinking it was this popobawa and he had come to do something terrible to me, something sexual. It is worse than what he does to women. I was fighting it."

The popobawa first appeared on Pemba, the smaller of Zanzibar's two main islands, around the time that the country's president was assassinated in 1972. Fear overcame shame as the popobawa instructed its victims that unless they told others of their ordeal it would be back. The island was in uproar as men went about announcing that they had been sodomized. After a few weeks the popobawa departed. There was another period of attacks in the 1980s, but nothing more until this April, when the winged beast swooped down on Zanzibar's largest island. Hamad was one of its earliest victims. He knew it was not a dream because when he woke his whole house was in uproar.

"I couldn't see it. I could only feel it. But some people in my house could see it. Those who've got the spirits in their head could see it. Everybody was terrified. They were outside screaming 'Huyo!' It means the popobawa is there. I had this bad pain in my ribs where it crushed me. Maybe it will attack anybody who doesn't believe," he warned.

When in Zanzibar, beware the popobawa!

There is no known protection against attack by the *popobawa* except for seeking safety in numbers. Whole families took to sleeping arm-in-arm in front of their houses.

Some said the *popobawa* took human form during the day. Fingers were pointed. A mentally ill man was hacked to death after inexplicably confessing he was the *popobawa*. The country's main hospital treated men with bruises, broken ribs and other injuries which the victims blamed on the creature. One month later, the *popobawa* disappeared.

Even skeptics admit that for true believers the attacks are real. Some attribute the return of the beast to times of political tension. The islands faced the uncertainty of elections and calls for self-government. The chief minister blamed the opposition for bringing the *popobawa*, while his op-

ponents responded by wondering if he himself might not be the creature.

GOTTA HAVE EWE

❦ A stuffed lamb is to be flown 10,000 miles because members of a remote tribe and their children want to see one for the first time. The tribe made the request after Bible-reading left them fascinated with the creatures. Missionaries contacted London's Natural History Museum; the museum contacted Wollaton Hall Museum in Nottingham, which has a collection of stuffed animals and shipped the woolly one all the way to Papua, New Guinea.

❦ Shane Patrick Neho, 17, and an associate broke into Barbarella's sex shop in Palmerston North, New Zealand, early on February 3. The two fled on bicycles, pursued by the public, dropping most of their loot, which included an inflatable sheep. "We have not yet ascertained why a sex shop should be stocking blow-up sheep," pondered Sergeant Ollie Outrim, "especially as Palmerston North has a large sheep population."

QUICKFOOT SIGHTED IN SCOTLAND FOREST

David Colman was driving down a country lane in West Lothian, Scotland, with his wife and three children when he saw what appeared to be a distinctly humanoid figure running down a forest

HEROIC ANIMALS

❂ Farmer Donald Mottram, 54, drove his four-wheeler into a field on his farm in Meidrim, Wales, to give a calf an injection. There was a bull 300 yards away, but he thought it was quiet, and was shepherding the injured calf when he was hit from behind. Man and motorcycle were hurled 30 feet. When he came to 90 minutes later, his herd—apparently marshaled by one of his favorite cows, 14-year-old Daisy—had surrounded him while the bull could be heard stamping the ground and bellowing. Mr Mottram, who weighs 240 pounds, crawled 200 yards to the gate while the herd shielded him. He was in the hospital for six days with broken ribs, damaged lungs and bruised shoulders. "They say cows are dumb creatures, but I'm certain my animals knew of the danger I was in and decided to protect me. Some of my favorite cows were in the group— as well as Daisy there was Megan, Amy, Bethan, Mary and Kitty. They undoubtedly saved me from being trampled to death."

❂ When her owner fell into a potentially fatal diabetic coma, a West Highland terrier called Holly came to the rescue. Holly fetched a bag of jellybeans, spilled two onto the floor by her owner's nose and then nuzzled her head to rouse her. Roz Brown, 45, of Cambridge, England, had suffered from diabetes for 38 years. The sugar in the sweets revived her and she was able to find two more in the bag before going in search of something more substantial. "I often have one if I feel unwell and Holly must have seen me eating them," she said.

❂ On August 16, a three-year-old boy fell 20 feet into the gorilla enclosure of Brookfield Zoo in suburban Chicago, landing on his head. Binti Jua, an eight-year-old Western Lowland gorilla with a baby on her back, headed off another gorilla. She then picked up the child, cradled him in her arms and placed him near a door where zookeepers could retrieve the boy, who recovered after a week in the hospital. Binti had been given ape-like stuffed dolls to play with in preparation for the birth of her own child. "I can't say that it was a typical response," said Melinda Pruett-Jones, curator of the gorilla department, "but there have been other instances where gorillas have shown maternal behavior to humans."

path at what seemed like 70 mph. This encounter with the "Quickfoot" happened in the Bathgate Hills, in an area known as Knock Forest.

When the mysterious and fleet-of-foot creature realized that it was being observed, it turned on Colman and his family and snarled. "It was about six feet tall with a human-like face," he said, "and seemed angry that we had disturbed it."

"My wife said, 'Did you see what I saw?'" The date of this event is not given, but Mr. Colman admitted to his interviewer: "It has taken me a long time to speak about this."

HOLLERS PROMPT HAIRY MANHUNT

In the summer of 1995, odd screams were heard up in the Blue Mountains which surround Walla Walla, Washington. Cattle began behaving oddly, as if disturbed by something. Resident Wes Sumerlin drove up into the mountains with Paul Freeman, a veteran Bigfoot hunter, and Bill Laughery, a former game warden, on August 4. They hiked in off Mill Creek Road and began the climb. Then Sumerlin got "a whiff of something, like somebody skinning muskrats."

They were in an area where they had seen Bigfoot tracks before. Sumerlin and Laughery reached a clearing, where they found a number of small trees twisted and broken, so fresh they were still dripping sap. There were large clumps of long hair, some black, some dark brown, caught on the trees where they were broken. They both caught sight of a seven-foot ape-like creature and heard the screams of two others. The creature was observed through binoculars at a distance of 90 feet, eating yellow wood and violets. The trackers also found droppings, two to five inches long, full of half-eaten carpenter ants, and fallen trees that had been pulled apart for the ants inside.

The hair clumps have been given to Frank Pourier, chairman of the anthropology department at Ohio State University, who is using a DNA test developed by the FBI for analysis of hair strands without roots. If the clumps turn out to come from an unknown primate, Pourier will compare them with a single hair reputed to be from the Chinese "wildman," given to him by Chinese peasants during a 1989 expedition. The latter does not match any known primate's hair, according to an analysis performed at Shanghai University.

YETI AGAIN

A yeti sighting in Kazakhstan has been reported by Pavel Marikovsky, an 80-year-old zoologist. The yeti, seen in mountains near Almaty, the capital, was "a terrifying, hairy being as tall as a fir tree but with very kind eyes."

BLOODSUCKER SPOOKS PUERTO RICO

This barbershop window warns of the "Goatsucker."

Reports of a red-eyed, hairy-armed beast which rips the organs from animals have spread fear on the Caribbean island of Puerto Rico. Known as Chupacabras, or "Goatsucker," the creature is blamed for the deaths of dozens of cats, dogs, cows, horses, turkeys, rabbits and goats, according to the police. Similar reports have surfaced since the 1970s.

The daily tabloid *El Vocero* reported that Chupacabras "sucked dead" five goats and 20 parakeets on Halloween. Angela Lajes found her dog and her sister's two cats dead in the southern city of Ponce in early November. Their guts were missing

THE SCHWASCAR AWARDS

CALL OF THE MILD

❤ A persistent canine phone caller was nabbed in November 1993. A woman in the midlands of England was sickened by many weeks of obscene slobbering and panting and called in British Telecom experts. The pesky pooch belonged to the woman's friend and had somehow learned to push a pre-recorded dial button.

RUNNERS-UP

❤ A specially trained Irish setter called Lyric saved the life of his asthmatic owner in Nashua, New Hampshire, on March 12 when she knocked the phone receiver off the hook, dialed 911 and barked into the mouthpiece. The oxygen mask of owner Judi Bayly had fallen off.

❤ Joan Soper left her mongrel Ben at home in Higham, England, for five minutes on April 21, 1993, while she stepped out to the shops. The five-month-old puppy knocked the phone to the floor and tapped out an emergency number. The operator heard heavy breathing and a dog barking; a dispatched policewoman peered through the mail slot and, spying blood on the phone, feared the worst. Eight more police soon arrived and smashed the door in with a sledgehammer only to find the house empty except for Ben, who was teething—the blood came from his gums.

❤ The following July in Lappeenranta, Finland, a German shepherd puppy made a similar connection. Staff at the emergency control center heard panting sounds which increased when they whistled, and they sent police to investigate. The staff's whistling seems the most puzzling part of this incident: can it be a tradition with Finnish law enforcement?

❤ Score one for the felines. Police in Boynton Beach, Florida, got an emergency call on Sunday night, January 12, 1992. The caller hung up without a word. They raced to the address, but no one answered. Another call from the same number arrived an hour later, followed by several more. Cops returned to the house and woke up Barbara Marple, who denied making the calls. It transpired that the culprit was her calico cat, named Kitten, who had punched 911 the first time and then hit the redial button.

❤ More recently, two dogs in Salisbury, England, dialed 999 on May 12. This operator took the gurgling and heavy breathing for a collapse victim's; police peering through the mail slot presumed a burglary had taken place. Upon notification, Carol Galpin rushed home to find a scene of chaos. Her Labrador cross-breeds had ransacked her home, yet managed to press each digit to reach the authorities: There was no speed-dial facility.

and they were drained of blood. In the latest reported incident, Goat-sucker was said to have opened the

This picture, allegedly of the Chupacabras, made the rounds on the Internet.

window of a house in the city of Caguas, destroyed a stuffed teddy bear and left a puddle of slime and a piece of rancid meat on the windowsill.

Mayor Jose Soto of Canovanas said his city of 40,000 had been visited by the beast 35 times. Other government officials said the animals had probably been killed by wild monkeys, but Soto retorted: "Monkeys don't suck blood. They don't steal organs."

WILD IDEAS

The Chinese government has launched a travel promotion as a prelude to a series of Wildman activities during 1997 in the Shennongjia region, Hubei Province, which has a park dedicated to the creature—whether it exists or not.

WATER MONSTERS

WHOLE LOCH OF SIGHTINGS GOING ON

Coach driver Jimmy Burnett claimed on March 8 that he and two busloads of pupils saw the Loch Ness monster on school runs 20 minutes apart. Burnett, who had driven the route for 30 years, noticed ripples and a hump and jumped from the bus with the nine pupils from Dochgarroch Primary School. Eilidh Barr, 11, said: "We saw a hump in the middle of the ripples, but we didn't see a head."

On April 16, Nessie was seen by Lancashire, England, disc jockey Bill Kinder, his wife and two children. He said: "It was shiny black, with a 30-foot-long trail in the water."

On June 13, Mrs. Kate Munro, who runs the Craigcarroch House Hotel beside Loch Ness with her husband, was walking with her daughter-in-law when at about 10 p.m. their attention was drawn to the water. "We saw a disturbance on the loch, a frothy disturbance with a wake tailing behind it," she said. "It would have been something large and it zigzagged quite a few times as an animal would do."

She went into the hotel and continued to watch it, joined by her husband Dave and 14 guests. The sighting lasted from five to ten minutes (reports differ), but nothing was seen on the surface. "There was no traffic on the loch at all," said witness David Neeld, "yet here was a wake as big as comes from a cruiser. I do not think there is any other explanation other than it was the Loch Ness monster."

MONSTER MACHINATIONS

Sweden's most famous monster, the Stoorjoodjuret (the monster of Lake Storsjön) may have been recorded on video by Gun-Britt Widmark, 67, while boating on the lake off Östersund with a party of retirees. Whatever it was had lumps and was 33–39 feet long.

"Every year we hear of people who have seen this beast," said Sten Rentzhog, president of the Östersund Society for the Scientific Investigation of Lake Storsjön, who has collected hundreds of sighting accounts dating back to 1635. "There are probably also a lot of witnesses who never tell anybody about their sightings, for fear of ridicule." The previous winter, the society obtained some detailed descriptions. "There are even people who have seen the beast while they were diving," said Rentzhog.

"Storsjoodjuret has been 'explained' in a number of ways—as ripples, gas bubbles, logs or misidentification of known animals—but none cover witnesses' descriptions adequately," says Rentzhog.

DINNER, NOT DINER

Deep-sea diver Cameron Turner, 27, discovered six bones 60 feet down at Loch Morar, in northern Scotland, during an expedition to the remote 1,077-foot deep loch. Initially, these were thought to be the remains of Morag, the monster reputed to live in the loch, first sighted in 1895; but they were later identified as deer bones.

"When I saw the bones poking through the silt on the loch bottom, I was sure they were from the tail of a water beast," commented Turner. "The only reason that they could have been so deep in the water is if they are the remains of Morag's dinner."

THE BEAST OF BENBECULA

An unidentified creature was photographed on the shores of Benbecula in the Hebrides of Scotland six years ago by Louise Whitts, a baby-sitter, when she was 16. Louise, of Bedlington, England, had always wondered what the creature was, but had never taken the photograph to an expert, believing she would look foolish when it was identified as a common sea creature. "It had what appeared to be a head at one end, a curved back and seemed to be covered with eaten-away flesh or even a furry skin and was about 12 feet long," she said. "It smelled absolutely disgusting, but the weird thing was that it had all these shapes like fins along its back—like a dinosaur or something."

When Louise moved out of her parents' home recently, she unearthed a photograph and took it to Alec Coles, curator and keeper of natural sciences at the Hancock Museum in Newcastle upon Tyne. On August 21, pictures of the creature were put on display at the museum. Mr. Coles said that none of the botanists, zoologists and marine biologists who had seen the pictures could throw any light on the puzzle.

IMPERSONATIONS

An owl has become addicted to television, according to a report from China. It was said to have flown into the home of farmer Zhang Liuyou in the southern Chinese province of Jiangxi one evening in April 1992; it perched on a beam and started watching television with the family. For the next three weeks, the bird came back, sometimes perching on the dinner table, and became hooked. The owl has since built a nest under the eaves of the house for daytime sleeping; at night, he returns to the beams or the table to watch the flickering screen.

The blackbirds of Guisborough, England, have learned how to imitate car alarms. "I started hearing this irritating noise outside at 5 a.m. every day," said journalist Mark Topping, 32. "It certainly seemed to be a car alarm, but there wasn't one close enough to be making that sort of row. Then I saw this one particular blackbird sitting in our alder tree, outside the bedroom window. It was giving it everything, but instead of the usual pleasant song of the blackbird it was re-creating the din made by a car alarm. After I heard that one bird I began to realize others had picked it up as well." David Hirst, a spokesman for the Royal Society for the Protection of Birds, explained that the birds had incorporated the sound into their song on the assumption that they were fellow birds requiring a response: "I've known them [to] imitate cellular phones and even cats."

DOGS AND CATS LIVING TOGETHER

❦ Fellene, a Chihuahua, suckles two stray kittens at Altaview Hospital, Salt Lake City, Utah. Tammy Dalton found the two abandoned kittens and put them in with her dog—even Fellene's six-week-old puppy Champ appears to have accepted his new siblings.

❦ And in Florida, Tiny, a four-year-old Chihuahua, is raising a kitten named Tiger. Tiny's owners Craig and Tim Lawson found Tiger abandoned on Vero Beach in June and their dog became a successful wet nurse to the feline orphan.

❦ Tisha, a 14-year-old King Charles spaniel, usually devoured any rabbits she caught; but after unearthing an orphaned litter of five baby rabbits, she brought them back to the New Zealand farm where she lives and produced milk to feed them.

❦ Shunned by other owls, Björk—an eagle owl chick at Twyford Wildlife Centre in Evesham, England—was pining to death until David and Michelle Buncle, who run the center, put her in with their cat Chiefly's new kittens. Chiefly accepted the owl as one of her own. Björk and the kittens play and sleep together and the sickly bird is now thriving.

SEA MONSTERS

In the first week of June, six giant cuttlefish were brought up in crab pots off Lowestoft in Suffolk, England. The largest measured 28 inches—more than twice the normal size.

FROM HULL OR HELL?

Glimpses of this cutie are rare.

A rarely seen sail-finned rough shark, two and a half feet long, black with large pointed teeth and a sandpaper feel to its skin, was dredged up by a Scottish fisherman and bought at a Hull, England, fishing market. It usually lives 800 feet down, out of reach of most nets. The University of Hull plans to preserve the ugly creature.

HORNED AND HAIRY TURKISH TERROR

Turkish officials sent investigators to the country's largest lake to look for a monster after several reported sightings. A parliamentary commission agreed to the search of Lake Van after Bestami Alkan, the provincial deputy governor, claimed to have seen the beast. "The monster was just like in cartoons," he said. "It was black and had triangular spikes on its back. It looked like a dinosaur." According to other witnesses interviewed by the commission, the monster's head "is black and hairy, and it has horns."

THE
NATURAL
WORLD

THE NATURAL WORLD

What with killer Komodo Dragon poop, orgasmic side effects from anti- (you-better-believe-it) depressants, and Yellowstone National Park's Old Faithful geyser failing to keep time, the Natural World, yet again, proved to be a veritable Petri dish of strangeness.

Biological and Medical weirdness took off enormously last year, thanks to NASA's announcement that they had discovered what appeared to be traces of bacterial life in Martian meteors. Crop Circles continue their dramatic slump—another hot summer with lots of people in the fields—Meteorological Superlatives were significantly up thanks to cold waves in the United States and heat and cold waves in Britain. Geophysical Activity was up, largely due to the spectacular volcanic eruptions in Iceland.

DISASTERS, NATURAL & MAN-MADE

FIRE IN THE MOUNTAINS

Experts of every stripe descended in January on Moirans-en-Montagne in the Jura mountains, France's toy-making capital, to investigate a mysterious "combustion wave." The trouble began on November 4, 1995, when Jean-Pierre Raffin's house in the rue de Cares burst into flames. At least 16 fires followed, in five different houses, all in the afternoon and all but four on a Saturday. Tins, garden furniture and cement bags ignited without apparent cause. The fires would often start in drawers or airing cupboards and often on metal objects.

Jean-Pierre's wife, Annie, died after three fires broke out within seven hours at the house on January 20; volunteer fireman Gerard David was also killed. Lab tests indicated this last fire burned at 2,400°F (chrome faucets had melted) and witnesses claimed that the orange flames had pointed into the wind. The fatalities suffered third-degree burns underneath intact clothing; the coroner said it was as if the victims had gone through a gigantic microwave oven.

On January 27, all the tiles on the roof of Madeleine Cordier's house fell off at once. Another blaze started in a wardrobe in the house of Jean-Pierre's brother, Charles, on the night of February 3. The local magistrate said that the scientists had failed to find any "electrical, nuclear or magnetic anomaly." Speculations included bombardment by satellite laser beams; seismic activity releasing inflammable gas from subterranean caves; electromagnetic pollution; and "leaking" from a 20,000-volt power line installed under the rue de Cares (scene of most of the fires) last July. Volcanologist Jean Meunier pointed out that Moirans rests on a geophysical fault line and suggested that ionized hydrogen was seeping out and igniting on contact with metal. A witch doctor from the Pyrenees Mountains said only a Vatican exorcist could save the town.

However, Pascal Raffin, 35, was caught on February 4 setting fire to a child's stroller in a garage near the house of his father, Charles, where the wardrobe had combusted the night before. After two days of interrogation, Raffin, nervous and quiet by nature, confessed to having set all the Moirans fires, but gave no reason. Allegedly, he used a very slow-burning chemical next to a highly inflammable material in confined places where the oxygen was thin, delaying ignition and allowing him time to get away. He also confessed to other fires in the neighborhood, such as the four that started within a period of four months at the barn of Rene Aquistapace two miles away. He remained very calm during questioning

PECULIAR PRESS

**PATIENT WITH BAD KNEE HAS
SURGERY ON HEALTHY TOOTH**
Times, September 14, 1995

WOMAN HAS BABY INSTEAD OF ULCERS
Lewiston (Maine) Sun-Journal, March 9, 1995

**RODENT TESTICLES MAY
FOIL REJECTION**
Rockland (New York) Journal-News,
October 15, 1995

and appeared to be detached from everything, according to a policeman.

But is the case solved? The explanation seems a bit too convenient for the authorities. The microwave-type third-degree burns, reminiscent of spontaneous human combustion, go unexplained.

TREE CAUSES MASSIVE CHAOS

Electricity and phone services were knocked out for up to five million people from Canada to Mexico after power lines failed in a rapid chain reaction on July 2. The blackout lasted between two and four hours. Hospitals from Seattle to San Diego faced crises and there was mayhem on the roads in 15 states. In San Francisco, the subway system was badly affected. Air conditioning was shut off as temperatures soared above 100°F in some areas.

A number of power stations were knocked off line—including four 500-megawatt coal-fired power plants at Rock Springs, Wyoming, the Hell's Canyon plant on the Snake River in Idaho and the Pawnee power plant in Brush, Colorado. Because the entire western third of the United States is essentially linked by one big power grid, the failure had a powerful ripple effect. It was the biggest blackout since the one in New York in 1977, which left eight million people without power for 36 hours.

On July 20, investigators announced that the blackout began with a transmission line short-circuiting when electricity jumped to a tree that had grown too close in a remote area about 100 miles east of the Kinport substation in southeastern Idaho. The initial outage, combined with record power demands during hot weather, led to a gigantic ripple effect. The tree was executed.

DISASTAIR

After three days of serious alloy talk, metallurgists attending a convention at the Cavendish Laboratory in Cambridge, England, gathered on the metal staircase for the end-of-conference photo. As the photographer raised the camera, the staircase fractured under their weight.

BIOLOGICAL AND MEDICAL

GALLING

Doctors removed 1,650 gallstones from a 47-year-old, Shanghai, China, woman in one operation.

SOBER WATER

A source of spring water that cures drunkenness has been found in Tarogsky Gorodok, in northwestern Russia. "Local men always attend the spring after weekends and holidays," said the Tass news agency. "The tale goes that some have even become tee-totalers, although no one has checked."

BUST BOUNCE

Dora Oberling, a stripper from Tampa, Florida, cheated death when a bullet fired at her by an irate 75-year-old member of the audience bounced off her silicone breast implants.

PARDON?

Family doctor Vincente Camara of Buenos Aires, Argentina, lost 90 percent of his hearing when a three-year-old boy screamed into his stethoscope as he examined him.

ROACH MOTEL

Swedish backpacker Magnus Carlstedt, 19, had a one-and-a-half-inch cock-roach pulled from his ear by ambulance men using tweezers. It had crawled in during the night in the Jolly Swagman hostel in Sydney, Australia.

WELL ENDOWED

Peruvian radio announcer Jose Vasquez, 25, who was born with two penises, has refused to let doctors remove one because "both are a gift of God." He claimed that his audience has soared since he told listeners about his unusual endowment.

YULE SPRIG PULLED FROM TEEN'S LUNG

Doctors in Stockton, California, found a one-inch sprig of Christmas tree in the right lung of Tracy McIntyre, 16. It had been there for almost 15 years, but was as green as ever. Since Christmas 1980, when 18-month-old Tracy suffered a choking fit near the tree, she's had breathing difficulties, coughing fits and bad breath. Finally her parents took her to a hospital.

THE LIVING DEAD OF SAN BERNARDO

San Bernardo, Colombia, is an agricultural town in the Andean foothills. Gravedigger Eduardo Cifuentes was the first to notice that the town's dead defied the normal process of decomposition when he began work 17 years ago. "The burial pit was full of bodies," he said. "I didn't like stepping on them because they were humans like us, so I started organizing them." (The custom was to remove mortal remains and transfer them to smaller urns five years after burial.)

Some of the mummies are housed in the underground crypt of the local cemetery. Though the smell of rotted flesh is strong, a dozen bodies are arranged in a standing position around the walls. Another dozen of the better-preserved mummies were moved in late 1994 to a new museum, or "pantheon," behind the cemetery, with an entry fee of about 500 pesos (55 cents). Here they are displayed on concrete slabs under glass. A man in an earth-colored suit next to the entrance greets visitors, a large wooden crucifix hanging from his neck underneath a smartly knotted tie. Three small children lie huddled together, one still wearing clothes and small white shoes, but with a large hole in the top of the doll-like head. Then there is Prudencia Acosta, dressed in a dark brown shawl and cape, clutching a red carnation in her claw-like hands. Some look peaceful and calm, while others are contorted with the grimaces of painful final moments.

Scientists can't explain this guy's composure.

Time has turned the mummies' clothes and skin to an earth-brown color. A few stand naked, exposing enlarged, dried-up genitals of uncommon size. A well-preserved severed hand lies on the head of one mummy, placed there for safekeeping after dropping off an arm. The best-preserved body stands neatly attired in a jacket, tie and trousers, with only an oddly pale face and sunken eye sockets to suggest he isn't with us anymore.

Scientists have examined the mummies, but are at a loss to explain the lack of decomposition. Local people claim the only other site in Latin America with natural mummification is the central Mexican town of Guanajuato, where villagers cite underground gas and soil conditions as the secret. In San Bernardo, however, the bodies are entombed above ground and do not come in contact with the earth. The locals offer a variety of explanations: the purity of the water; the fact that the cemetery attracts solar radiation; the lack of chemical additives in the food; or the fact that people eat a lot of *guatila* and *balu*.

"Some people say they are not going to have a bunch of kids coming along and poking fun at their dead relatives," said Claudia Garcia, a San Bernardo resident. "If they see that the body has mummified when it is disinterred, they ask for it to be chopped up with a machete or an axe and then burnt. Sometimes they watch to make absolutely sure the body is cut up properly."

CURIOUS CORPSE

Chinese scientists are baffled by a corpse that has failed to decompose or turn stiff three and a half years after the old woman died. Not only had the body not rotted away, the face of the corpse was still radiant, many of its joints still supple, and the head still turned on its shoulders.

The woman, from Hubei Province, died of heart failure in November, 1992. Her grandson said that her temperature was normal and her muscles flexible ten hours later. Rigor mortis had still not set in after two days, so the family decided to keep the body. After three years the body

THE SCHWASCAR AWARDS

TINY TWIN

❤ A small four-year-old boy was admitted to the Tansen Mission Hospital in Katmandu, Nepal, in January 1993, complaining of an expanding mass in his upper abdomen. A swelling had been present since the child was born, but it was increasing in size and causing persistent vomiting. When doctors operated they discovered a large sac which contained a 13.8-inch fetus with umbilical cord and placenta: Here was a classic case of foetus in foetu. The boy made a full recovery. A similar operation was reported on a 17-year-old youth in New Delhi the day before.

RUNNERS-UP

❤ On September 21, 1992, doctors at the Sarjito state hospital in Yogyakarta, central Java, operated on six-month-old Adnan Sukmana to remove the fetus of his twin from his abdominal cavity.

❤ An ultrasound test on a Saudi boy born in August 1994 with a swollen stomach showed an unidentifiable body inside him. When he was four months old, an operation discovered "three fetuses stuck behind the stomach, on the pancreas and a part of the colon," according to Dr. Talal al-Maliki, a pediatrician in the town of Assir.

❤ Huang Juyu, 59, a farmer from Jiangsu Province in China, went to see a doctor in 1994 suffering severe stomachache and weight loss. An operation removed the underdeveloped fetus of his twin from his bladder.

❤ Doctors in the Egyptian city of Sohag found two fetuses in the abdomen of a baby boy last summer. They operated on Ahmed Mohammed for five hours to remove a deformed fetus and part of another.

---

had still not decomposed despite fluctuations in the temperature ranging from freezing to 93°F.

WILD MEDICINE

Chimpanzees foraging in the wild were seen to go to a lot of trouble to select leaves and hold them in their mouths. One leaf from a shrub called aspilia contained a compound that killed roundworm. "It was a sort of extraordinary, bizarre molecule that no synthetic organic chemist would ever think of making," said Philip Whitfield of Kings College, London. "It happens to be a very good drug."

EAGLE EYES

Unnamed scientists in Madagascar claim that Besilo Maramoko, 83, has the best eyesight in the world because he can read a newspaper from 32 feet.

IN BLACK AND WHITE

A mother has given birth to twins, one black and one white. Michelle Hamilton, 31, has a black father and a white mother and the twins' father, Robert Calvert, is black. The babies were delivered by Caesarean section on June 27, one month premature, at St. George's Hospital in London. Jolene, who is white, weighed five pounds, two ounces and Robert Jr., who is black, four pounds and six ounces. "One of my other daughters was born white, but has grown darker," said Ms. Hamilton, who has four older children.

LATE DELIVERIES

❧ A woman who died at 92 had been carrying her dead baby—long since calcified—for 60 years. The fetus was discovered after the woman went to a Vienna, Austria, hospital suffering from senile dementia and pneumonia; she had a large abdominal mass extending from the pelvis to the right upper abdomen. Radiography showed lithopaedion (a stone child). When the woman died a week later, the autopsy revealed that the baby had reached 31 weeks gestation. The woman's son said she had become pregnant for the fourth time at 32, developed abdominal pain and then recovered. Her menstrual periods resumed. She had no subsequent serious illness, apart from infertility.

The earliest documented case of a stone child comes from a 1200 B.C. grave in the United States. This complication of extrauterine pregnancy is now very rare because ectopic gestation escapes surgical treatment less frequently than before. Stone children now occur once in 250,000 pregnancies. The body forms calcium on dead tissue which is too large to be absorbed. This latest case was probably the longest time a woman had carried a calcified fetus.

❧ Irene McCarthy, 62, of Wheeling, West Virginia, sought medical treatment for stomach pains. X rays revealed a shriveled eight-inch extrauterine fetus lodged near her appendix. She was pregnant at the age of 18 in 1952 and went into labor, but no child was born. She had been carrying the fetus for 41 years. As it was unconnected with her stomach pains, she declined to have it removed.

❧ The skeleton of a fetus was removed from the womb of a Burmese woman after it had been there 19 years. The operation was conducted at Al Dar Private Hospital in Madinah, Saudi Arabia, by Dr. Islam Abdul Moneim. He said that half of the woman's womb was removed as it was found to be adhered to the colon and intestines. The baby had died just a week before the due delivery date.

LIVIN' LARGE

Builders in Brooklyn removed a bay window and several rows of bricks on May 18 so that a 1,000-pound man could be taken to a hospital to save his life. Michael Hebranko, 43, who put on hundreds of extra pounds in the few months after he lost control of his eating addiction, was critically ill with heart and respiratory problems, and gangrene. Possibly the heaviest person alive, he is way under the official record of 1,400 pounds, held by the late John Brower Minnoch of Bainbridge Island, Washington.

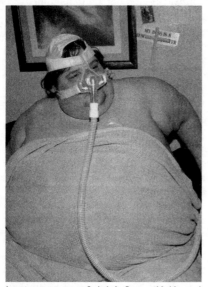

Awaiting transport to St. Luke's–Roosevelt's Hospital, Mr. Hebranko was given immediate medical care.

For nine weeks Hebranko had been unable to stand for more than 30 seconds and was confined to a sofa in his living room, covered in a blanket because none of his clothes would fit his 110-inch waist. A team of 20 paramedics lifted him through the hole in the wall on a stretcher used to transport small whales, after which he was loaded into the ambulance with a fork-lift.

Mr. Hebranko lost 705 pounds in 1989 and appeared in Deal-a-Meal diet advertisements; but in 1994 he lapsed and gained more weight than ever.

RIGHT UNDER OUR NOSES

Some mysteries are closer than you would expect. Two dentists at the University of Maryland have discovered a jaw muscle overlooked by surgeons for 500 years. It might explain links between sore jaws and pain behind the eyes. Gwendolyn Dunn and Gary Hack were studying temporomandibular joint (TMJ) disorder (the painful clicking in the lower jaw where it articulates with the skull). Anatomy books only showed the joint from the side, so they dissected a cadaver face-first and found the unknown one-and-a-half-inch-long muscle running between the jaw and a bony knob behind the eye socket. They have since seen it in dozens of cadavers.

Finding a new muscle in the human head is like finding an overlooked elephant in the living room. Surgeons have noticed this strip of tissue, but described it incorrectly as an extension of the temporalis, a muscle running from the side of the head. The two muscles are not only physically separated but distinct in every way, with separate nerves and blood supply. The muscle, known so far only as "he," is one of five involved in chewing, and the researchers believe it must help to lift and support the jaw.

BIG BOY

Zack Strekert looks like a miniature Sumo wrestler. At 17 months, he weighs almost 68 pounds, as much as a nine-year-old. He is three feet tall and nearly as big around. His ankles won't fit into shoes and on hot days he wears nothing but a diaper, in the largest adult size. No evidence of a glandular disorder has been found. The diagnosis was "morbid obesity," but his mother Laurie, 29, said he had never been a big eater. "He'll have a quarter-cup of cereal for breakfast, crackers for a snack and half a sandwich for lunch." He weighed a mere ten pounds, twelve ounces at birth.

I'M FEELING MUCH BETTER, DOCTOR

The antidepressant clomipramine (brand name Anafranil) is giving some users an uplifting bonus: when they yawn, they have an orgasm. The *Canadian Journal of Psychiatry,* back in 1985, said that one woman, cured of her depression, asked if she could continue to use the drug since she enjoyed the side effect so much. She could even experience an orgasm by deliberately yawning. Another patient, a man, solved the "awkward and embarrassing" problem of repeated spontaneous climaxes by wearing a condom all day. According to several research papers, some five percent of users report the side effect, which has also been observed in some Prozac users—although for most people the drugs inhibit the ability to reach orgasm.

PICK YOUR BRAINS

Troy Harding, 19, bumped into the tip of his car's radio antenna in Portland, Oregon, on May 29, 1995. About three inches of the antenna went up his nose, pierced his sinus, entered his brain and hit his pituitary gland. He managed to pull himself free, but lost about one pint of blood. A week later, he found standing still gave him a headache.

CYSTER

A woman who couldn't fit behind the steering wheel of her car thought she was hopelessly fat until it was discovered she was carrying a 91-pound fluid-filled ovarian cyst. On February 16, doctors at St. Joseph's Women's Hospital in Tampa, Florida, drained eight gallons of blood from the benign cyst, which had displaced organs in the abdomen. The 27-year-old woman is five feet, four inches tall and has been heavy since the age of 12.

The largest ovarian cyst on record weighed 328 pounds and was drained and removed in Texas in 1905. The largest ever removed intact weighed 303 pounds; this was from a 34-year-old woman in Stanford, California, in 1991.

WHEN NAIR WON'T DO

Abys DeJesus, a two-year-old girl from Puerto Rico, suffers from congenital hairy nævus, allegedly once known as "human werewolf syndrome," a potentially fatal condition. She has a mask of dense brown hair over her nose and half her face. There are 23 smaller patches of hair on her body. Her condition is similar in appearance but apparently unrelated to the "werewolf gene," a disorder that affects males in a single Mexican family. Abys lives mostly indoors, sheltered from other children, who often run in fear from her. No one else in her family has the condition.

Dr. Adrian Lo of St. Christopher's

Hospital in Philadelphia began a three-month procedure on August 27 which he hopes will remove the hair by inflating the unblemished skin and grafting it over the surgically cleaned area. The result is expected to be smoother and more natural than a traditional skin graft, which can leave puckers and valleys.

SUTURE SELF

Doctors in Malawi were mystified by the reappearing stitches which plagued Opani Banda, 14. The sutures were removed at a hospital in central Nkhotakhota on November 17, but they reappeared the following morning. She returned to the hospital to have them removed again, but by mid-afternoon they had reappeared a second time at random on the left side of her body.

"This is the power of witchcraft," said orthopedic officer Philip Mayendayenda. "If it is not, then it could be the work of people from outer space." The sutures appeared nylon or wire-like in texture, he said.

The family had consulted a witch doctor, but he had failed to get rid of the stitches.

MORE SEEDS OF TIME

Tiny crustacean eggs that lay buried under sediment at the bottom of Bullhead Pond in Perryville, Rhode Island, since about 1639, have been hatched after exposure to fluorescent "daylight" at about 16 degrees below zero.

The offspring belong to a copepod or paddlefoot called *Diaptomus sangineus,* a near-microscopic, teardrop-shaped animal with long antennae. Professor Nelson Hairston of Cornell University retrieved the eggs on August 23, 1990. According to his report

in the journal *Ecology* last September, the newly hatched larvae produced further eggs at the appropriate point in their 12-stage life cycle. More than half of the 355-year-old eggs hatched; Hairston was also able to hatch some nearly 400 years old eggs. Although it was known that spores of 135-million-year-old single-celled organisms could be viewed, scientists believe this is the first time a multi-celled creature has been brought to life after several centuries.

HIGH DRAMA

Professor Andrew Wallace of Queen's Medical Centre, Nottingham, England, received the Weigelt Wallace Prize for extraordinary dedication to medicine after performing lifesaving surgery in an airplane. Dr. Wallace was aboard a 707 traveling to London from Hong Kong on May 22, 1995, when passenger Pauline Dixon, 39, complained of chest pains. He recognized that Dixon, who had been in a motorcycle crash on the way to the airport, had several fractured ribs and a collapsed lung. With the aid of Dr. Tom Wong from Tayside, England, Dr. Wallace took a scalpel and local anesthetic from the aircraft's emergency kit and cut into Dixon's chest as she lay in row 53 of economy class. Dr. Wong held the wound open with a knife and fork sterilized in five-star brandy. Wallace inserted a chest drain made from a urinary catheter, also sterilized in brandy, and strengthened with a coat hanger and held in place with cellophane tape. The air pocket on her left lung was drained out through a mineral water bottle adapted as a one-way valve. The ten-minute operation was successful, and by the time Flight 32 landed twelve hours later, Dixon was well enough for breakfast.

GETTING THE POINT

❂ If you go abroad, make sure you have health insurance. Ulrich Schild, a 39-year-old German tourist in the Dominican Republic, didn't; the wonder is that he lived to regret it. Ulrich and his girlfriend Michelle Sujatta were traveling on a rented motorcycle when it spun out of control. He was flung through the air and impaled on a branch which broke off with the force of the impact.

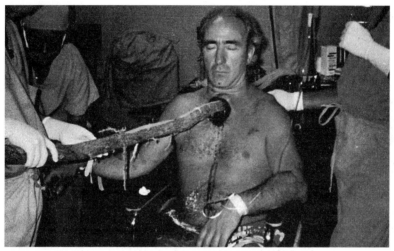

Ulrich Schild waited for three hours in a Dominican Republic hospital while they wrangled over his medical bill.

Michelle managed to flag down a passing car. Still conscious and with nearly five feet of branch protruding from the top center of his chest, Ulrich was taken to a nearby clinic. The clinic said they had no facilities to treat him, and recommended the hospital in the city. Though in shock, Ulrich somehow found the strength to continue. At the hospital, doctors quickly injected Ulrich with painkillers—but when they learned that he had no travel insurance, they refused to operate without cash.

Luckily for Ulrich, a compromise was eventually reached. The hospital demanded a letter from the German embassy confirming that they would cover the cost of the treatment. He then had to wait for more than three hours—as a kebab—while an embassy official could be located to sign the letter. Finally, Ulrich, still conscious, was wheeled into an operating room where surgeons removed the branch.

He had been very lucky. The stake had missed his heart and emerged to the left of his spine. "When I woke up and found I was not paralyzed, I knew I would recover."

EPIDEMICS AND ILLNESS

GETTING THE POINT

❦ Logger Alexander Ivanov, 34, was skewered through his abdomen by the top of a felled tree in northern Russia. Colleagues who had witnessed the accident quickly trimmed the tree to a six-foot stake. An Onega hospital removed the stake, and internal damage was repaired in Arkhanngelsk; Ivanov recovered well.

❦ Gas worker Graham Blakeway, 43, was cleaning a gas main in Sandal, England, when he dislodged a 20-foot-long, spring-loaded rod. The rod was released with such force that it pierced a thick rubber mat; a ten-foot section shot through his abdomen. As firemen used hydraulic cutting gear to chop the rod on both sides, Blakeway asked for a message to be sent to his wife—to tape his favorite TV program. He recovered fully.

❦ Steve Reeder, a 29-year-old hotel worker in Scarborough, England, has twice been impaled on fenceposts and lived. His latest accident happened when the car in which he was a passenger skidded off a road, throwing him onto wooden railings. A 30-foot section spiked him through the armpit and passed through his shoulder. It took 40 minutes for rescue workers to unpin him from his seat, but after just a few hours in the hospital he was allowed home. The earlier accident happened when he was 14 years old and fell off his bike.

ALLERGIC TO COMPUTERS

Retired secretary Joan Stock of Saltford, England, suffers a severe reaction to the high frequency emissions from microchips. She discovered her affliction in 1975 when her employers installed a new electronic typewriter at her desk. "Within a few minutes I had severe pains in my ears, like hot wires piercing them. Then acute head pains."

She now has to travel in old cars, use manual typewriters and a 20-year-old television, and avoid bank ATMs. She wears a special battery-powered pendant which sends electromagnetic pulses into her body at a rate tailored to her needs.

PLAGUE BY RUMOR

According to a report last December by the department of epidemiology and infectious diseases of the Swiss Federal Office for Public Health, the apparent outbreak of plague in India in the autumn of 1994 was an "epidemic in the media" rather than a medical reality. The office concludes with sarcasm that "an attentive reader would have observed that the plague disappeared from the press on October 5, 1994, the day of the Solar Temple massacre [in Switzerland]."

The panic was triggered by a news item about pneumonic plague in Surat on September 26; 100,000 people fled the city. The diagnosis seemed to be supported by the first blood tests, and victims had the swollen lymph nodes associated with the disease. Several countries severed air links with Calcutta, western tourists returning from India were subject to examinations and the Indian economy lost some $950 million in a few days.

The World Health Organization confirmed, after an on-the-spot study, that *Yersinia pestis*, the bug responsible for plague, was found in neither man nor animal in India during the period concerned.

CLASS TRIPS

A mystery ailment causing students to hallucinate, shout, wail and hurt themselves affected 27 pupils out of 1,000 at the Tamale Business Secondary School in the northern Ghanaian town of Tamale in June. It was temporarily closed. According to the June 26 *Ghanaian Times,* 11 pupils at two other secondary schools in the town had been treated for similar symptoms in the previous four days. The victims said they had visions of an old lady beckoning them. "Experts" said the condition might be caused by drugs such as marijuana and cola nuts!

TOP OF THE POX

The world was declared smallpox-free in 1979 and destruction of the remaining stocks of the virus has been recommended by a World Health Organi-

GREAT BALLS OF FIRE

❦ People living in central Japan were agog on the afternoon of January 7 as they watched a fireball accompanied by a loud noise and a white plume of smoke. One eyewitness said: "An orange object with sparks following it fell to the southeast and it looked like a huge firework going off." Shortly afterward, Ryutaro Araki, 19, found what appeared to be a fragment of a meteorite in Tsukuba, a town northeast of Tokyo. The fragment landed about 55 yards ahead of him while he was driving and it was warm when he picked it up. It resembled half an egg, measuring two inches by more than an inch and weighing about two ounces.

❦ Dozens of motorists on a Scotland highway jammed police switchboards on February 13 to report sightings of a fireball, said to be the size of a large house, which left a blazing trail along the horizon before splitting in two and landing in fields. A Lothian and Borders police spokesman said that there was no evidence of any object having crashed in the area concerned. A Civil Aviation Authority spokesman said they had no record of the fireball. Ron Halliday, chairman of Scottish Earth Mysteries Research said it was far too big to have been a meteor.

❦ A meteor streaked a path across the evening sky on February 6 from central Massachusetts to Rhode Island, leaving a bright, bluish trail behind as it disappeared over the Atlantic. The object turned orange as it reached the eastern horizon. Sightings were reported from 5:20 p.m. to 5:35 p.m.

CIRCLES CROP UP ALL OVER EUROPE

As these photos prove, England is still the world's leading producer of cornography. Nevertheless, other locations in Europe have also witnessed enigmatic crop-crushings. On July 13, three circles, 41, 30 and 15 feet in diameter, appeared in Podmokly in the Czech Republic; five days later, two more, 67 and 12 feet in diameter, were found in a field in the nearby town of Susice. Lubos Safarik, secretary of the Psychotronic and UFO club, based in Plizen (Pilsen), has researched 14 formations in the country since the spring of 1994, and believes they are made by "some form of higher intelligence." In Holland, a double-circle formation appeared in Dalem, about 16 miles south of Utrecht.

This spectacular arrangement turned up in a Barnes, England barley field.

More than 150 circles went into this pattern, located near Stonehenge, England.

This Rosette motif is composed entirely of barley.

This "tailed circle" is a recurrent icon in crop circles.

zation panel, a move that would mark the first deliberate extinction of a biological entity. D-day was penciled in for June 30, 1999, pending approval by the 190-nation World Health Assembly. The virus stocks, kept frozen in liquid nitrogen in Atlanta and Novosibirsk, were originally scheduled for destruction in 1990, and two deadlines for ex-ecution—December 31, 1993, and June 30, 1995—passed by after objections led by the U.K.'s Chemical and Biological Defense Establishment at Porton Down. The argument went that if any nations had secret stocks of the virus for use in biological warfare, the original virus would be needed to prepare a new vaccine.

THE AWFUL TOOTH

The first recorded AIDS transmission by a human bite was confirmed on October 27, 1995. It happened in West Palm Beach, Florida, when prostitute Naomi Morrison bit Elmer Hutto, 91, while trying to steal his wallet. Researchers said the infection was not transmitted through saliva but from blood in the woman's mouth, because she had bleeding gums.

ANOTHER REASON TO STOP EATING CHIMP

The Ebola virus claimed the lives of 13 people in Gabon, West Africa, in February after a dead chimpanzee was eaten at a feast in the remote village of Mayibout. Seven people infected with the virus had been admitted to the hospital in Makokou and seven others were under observation. The authorities were trying to trace those who had helped to bring the sick to the hospital. A number of dead animals were found near Mayibout and neighboring villages, including a second chimpanzee, a wild cat, an antelope and two gorillas.

Ebola, which causes extensive internal and external bleeding, kills at least 70 percent of the people it infects. The virus was named after the River Ebola in northern Zaire where it first appeared in 1976. There was an outbreak in and around Kikwit, Zaire, in May 1995 which killed 245 people, and a case in the Ivory Coast last December, but the victim survived.

MORE THAN DOUBLE YOUR PLEASURE

A rumor circulating in the Egyptian town of Mansura, 81 miles northeast of Cairo, maintains that women are being driven to sexual frenzy after chewing gum laced with aphrodisiacs peddled by agents of Israel. The local minister of Parliament, Fathy Mansour, has accused Israel of "a huge scheme to ravage the young population of Egypt." He said the effects of the gum lasted about two hours.

The tale proved irresistible for several of Egypt's feisty, and often wildly inaccurate, opposition newspapers. One named the Russian emigré chemist who allegedly concocted the evil substance on behalf of Mossad, Israel's intelligence service.

Israel is still regarded with suspicion by the vast majority of Egyptians even after 17 years of peace, and has long been blamed as source of "corrupting influences," including smuggled pornographic videos, hormone-laced fruit and furtively peddled aphrodisiacs. Yet analysis by Egypt's Ministry of Health found nothing in the brands of so-called Israeli gum, traced to smugglers in Gaza, that could stimulate sexual arousal, according to the health minister, Ismail Sallam; and an investigation by the vice squad in al-Daqahlya Province found nothing to back up Fathy Mansour's assertion that 15 women had sexually assaulted their male classmates after chewing the gum.

PECULIAR PRESS

MEXICAN LEADER CRASHES TO EARTH
Guardian, December 28, 1994

SWEDISH JET HIJACKED BY A BREAD ROLL
International Herald Tribune, June 29, 1995

HEADS FLY TO FUNERAL
Daily Mirror, November 6, 1995

Still, loudspeakers in Mansara blared warnings against chewing gum, announcements that had been a standard feature of Friday sermons for some weeks. The authorities banned the suspected gum, closed kiosks and arrested dealers for trafficking in smuggled goods. Citizens were convinced: "We are no longer safe," said Sayada Abdul Moneim, a 20-year-old high school graduate. "I now chew a brand of gum that is made in Egypt. It is not very good quality, but at least it is safe."

For many, prudence lost out. A university official at the Youth and Sports Affairs Department said that several young women had made gum-related sexual confessions. "We women are very weak," said the official, who insisted on anonymity. "Anything like that gum could affect us."

"I lived the experience deeply and truly," said a 21-year-old identified only as Amira, explaining that she had accepted a ride and then a piece of gum from two male classmates. "At the beginning, I thought that this feeling was just because I was alone with them in the the the car," the woman said. "But gradually, I was beginning to wish that one of them was in the back seat. I was so easy. I found no resistance. And you know the rest."

GROWIN' UP TOO FAST

Eleven children from a remote village in the mountains of central Mexico suffer from Cockayne's syndrome, a rare illness that causes premature aging and slow death. Six of them arrived for treatment in the city of Puebla on May 22. There have been fewer than 150 victims of the illness registered since its discovery by British doctor E. A. Cockayne in 1936. The condition arises from genetic aberrations resulting from inbreeding.

In the village of San Martin Toxpalan (population 2,800), two brothers named Carrera founded three generations who in turn intermarried among cousins and siblings. The stricken six, all first cousins between the ages of two and 23, are descendants of the Carrera brothers. Their skin is wrinkled, they are mentally retarded and their hearing, sight, bones and muscles are those of the very old.

DRAGON DUNG DISASTER

When 50 people fell ill with a potentially fatal salmonella infection in January after visiting the Denver Zoo, the Center for Disease Control and Prevention was called in. Eight of the stricken were hospitalized and one victim was seriously ill for nearly four weeks.

State epidemiologist Richard Hoffman said that the victims had all visited a special exhibit featuring giant Komodo dragons and had not washed their hands before eating or leaving the zoo.

Curiously, it was those who touched the wooden enclosure of the "Dragon Days" exhibit—rather than those who actually touched the lizards— who became infected. Hoffman said the reptiles had defecated in mulch in the enclosure, then walked around, spreading the bacteria to the wooden barriers.

One of the zoo's four Komodo dragons tested positive for a type of salmonella that is common and these bacteria's unusual appearance clearly established the link between the victims and the exhibit.

FALLS FROM THE SKY

SOMETHING FISHY

Falls of fishes are few and far between these days, but a splendid example happened on May 17. The incident occurred at Hatfield, England, at about 6:30 p.m., as Mrs. Ruth Harnett and her husband, David, were hurrying to unload the weekly shopping. It was not raining and the air became suddenly very chilly. Hearing a loud thump on her van's roof, Ruth was surprised to see a modest-sized fish. Looking up into the cloudy sky, she saw a second fish heading toward her. It hit the van's hood.

"I looked around, thinking it was kids mucking about," said Ruth. "Then three more fish dropped on my garden and I realized they were falling from the sky." She called David, who was inside the house. "As he came out, I looked up again, which was a big mistake. I was bombarded with fish and one hit me in the face." Some local children came running up laughing and they all stood in wonder as about 20 more fish plummeted earthward.

Their clothes covered in scales, they gathered the two- to five-inch-long fishes. The fish were thought to be young roach, rud or dab and weighed four pounds altogether. Although they were dead, the fish seemed fresh and warm to the touch, as though heated by the sun in their aerial travels.

This was the second time in living memory that Ruth's family had experienced this strange phenomenon. "I remember as a child my father telling me that his father was caught in a shower of fishes and frogs near Welwyn Garden City, just seven miles away, about 60 years ago."

SNOW DRIFTS

Passersby were showered with heroin which collected in drifts outside a Hong Kong public housing estate in April 1996. A man and a woman tossed more than 11 pounds of the drug, wrapped in plastic, out of a 16th floor window when police burst in.

WATER BOMB

Two pilots of an Italian firefighting plane were placed under investigation after dropping thousands of liters of water on a flotilla of small boats participating in a pageant. The pageant, held near the Sardinian tourist resort of Villasimius, was for the feast of Our Lady of the Shipwrecked; ten people were injured and several boats capsized.

PLANE PELLET

A three-inch metal rod, one inch in diameter, came within inches of killing production-line worker John MacGregor when it crashed through the roof of the Symphony Furniture factory in Leeds, England, in early March 1995. Symphony's technical manager Donald Abbott thought it must have come from an airplane: "There are shear marks on the rod where it has broken off something, and we are on the flightpath for Yeadon. It must have been traveling fast when it came through the roof. It could have been fatal." Yet Rob Lund, operations director at Yeadon Airport, said: "All aircraft . . . are checked routinely by their captains

THE SCHWASCAR AWARDS

FALL GUY

❦ Pat Dolan, 38, was paragliding over the Dolemite Mountains in Italy when he hit an "asymmetrical tuck" which caused his parachute to collapse and wrapped his reserve chute around his body. He fell from a height of 6,500 feet in a standing position, with both arms strapped to his side. Fortunately, a lone snowdrift broke Dolan's 100-mph approach; amazingly, he suffered only three crushed vertebrae and fractures to his right leg and heel. The medical specialists treating the paraglider's injuries were equally astonished at his fast healing. Dolan is expected to walk again.

RUNNERS-UP

❦ In May 1995, a group of maintenance workers on the Clifton Suspension Bridge in Bristol, England, got a shock when they saw 36-year-old Chris Copus fall past them. They were even more shocked when they saw that he was still moving after his 245-foot fall to the Avon River. Conscious throughout his rescue, Copus came out of the ordeal with arm, leg and collarbone fractures, but no lasting injuries; footage from the bridge's security cameras later suggested that Copus had been saved by the wind catching his raincoat.

❦ In October 1995, 18-month-old Grant Huff of Encinitas, California, was playing in his grandmother's garden when he managed to crawl over a two-foot wall. In the neighbor's yard, Huff slipped and rolled 30 feet down a steep cliff before falling 50 feet into the Pacific Ocean. Promptly found by a couple on the beach, Huff spent a night in the hospital, but was discharged the following day, as he suffered absolutely no injuries.

❦ In 1994, the entire Preston family of Tynemouth, England, survived a 50-foot plunge onto a North Tyneside beach—in their Nissan. Following a collision, the Prestons' car crashed through iron safety rails, fell sideways down a 45-degree slope, hit a concrete wall, fell a further five feet, and finally came to rest on a wall with its rear in the air. The passengers were all completely unhurt, though the car was totaled. One witness said: "I couldn't believe it when the doors opened and they all got out. People started running towards them, but they didn't really need any help."

❦ In March 1996, three-year-old Oscar Blaxland fell from his parents' fifth-floor apartment in Sydney, Australia. He came through the 65-foot fall practically unhurt. A paramedic who treated Blaxland on the scene says he was conscious with no visible injuries, only complaints of "soreness." After a week in the hospital for observation, the youngster was released.

and engineers and nothing has been found to be missing." He said it must have come off some other aircraft flying over the factory.

HEAVEN SENT

One year ago, the tribesfolk of Kotorigu in Ghana's remote West Mamprusi district gathered in trepidation to worship a strange object with a garish orange parachute that had hit the savannah and set the bush ablaze. The chief ordered his eldest son to stand guard beside it, without a break, for five days and five nights. The Ghanaian Times suspected the object to be the handiwork of aliens, reporting that the parachute had unusual inscriptions. These later proved to be Russian trademarks.

The object was in fact a Russian-built satellite called Express, launched from Japan on January 15, 1995, as part of the German-Japanese space program. At a height of 93 miles its second-stage rocket (made in Japan) misfired, leaving it in orbit 62 miles lower than intended. At the time of writing, the German space agency DARA was negotiating with the Ghanaian government in Accra for the return of the $45 million gizmo— Germany's most important space experiment. It had managed only two and a half orbits, returning to earth from its planned five-day mission four days and 21 hours early. German mission control had expected it to splash down in the Pacific, but were some 7,400 miles wide of the mark. It was last seen by a tracking station in Santiago, Chile, and was only traced months later through the German ambassador in Accra.

WHAT GOES UP

While the Chinese navy was conducting threatening war games with live missiles off the coast of Taiwan, the derelict Chinese spy satellite Jianbing, about the size of a small car, red hot and traveling at about 1,000 mph, plunged harmlessly into the South Atlantic 1,000 miles southeast of Brazil in the early hours of March 12. It was encased in oak paneling to protect it against the heat of reentry. Two days before splashdown, it was passing over the U.K. four times a day and the chance of its landing there (and destroying everything within 300 feet) was said to be 70:1. Its last orbit was tracked over eastern Florida, Trinidad and Tobago, and then disappeared out of radar sight. One of the FSW-1 series, it was launched in October 1993, but its rockets misfired after ten days, sending it into a "decaying" elliptical orbit and making inevitable a premature return to earth.

A GIFT FROM ABOVE

Shirley Tovell found a freshwater crayfish in the flowerbed of her home at Alexandra Park, England. As she lies about two miles from the nearest river or sea, the mystery was how it got there. The consensus of consulted wildlife experts was that it had been dropped by a heron or gull.

FROGSTORM

Nellie Straw, of Sheffield, England, said that, as she and her family headed for Loch Lomond in their car on the

STRANGE DEATHS

☻ A Bauma, Austria, man accidentally killed his two-year-old daughter by building a snowman on top of her. Dozens of neighbors joined the search for the girl, identified only as Priscilla, when she was discovered missing from the playground in front of the family's home. One person noticed something strange about the snowman and uncovered the child curled up underneath and blue in the face.

☻ Two beachcombers found a block of ice encasing the naked corpse of a man at Roedvig, southeastern Denmark. Police didn't think the man, aged 20–25 and with Asian features, was murdered as there were no signs of wounds. They also considered suicide unlikely, as suicides don't usually strip. The body had been in the ice for several weeks.

☻ The body of Henry Carlton, 41, was found on February 5 wedged halfway through the basement window of a real estate agency in Williamsport, Pennsylvania. His legs were inside and his head and arms outside, and a bag of burglary tools was next to him. He apparently believed he could squeeze through the 15-inch-high, 18-inch-wide window and drop to the floor; but the window was obstructed by a heating duct and Carlton's bulky clothes stopped him. He froze to death.

A82, a "terrible storm" caught them between Crianlarich and Glencoe. "All of a sudden frogs began to fall on the car, hundreds of them. We couldn't believe our eyes."

TEARS OF THE GODS

All hail!

An enormous teardrop of ice, weighing four pounds, fell out of the sky and landed on a grass verge near stunned commuters at a bus stop in Ecclesfield, England. Firemen took it back to the Tankersley fire station and preserved it in a freezer. Later, someone took it out and dropped it.

SURROUND SOUND

A tornado tore through Ontario and blew away a drive-in theater in St. Catharines showing the movie *Twister*. There were no reports of casualties, but trucks were thrown around like toys and trailers were "smashed to smithereens."

METEOROLOGICAL SUPERLATIVES

ON THE ROCKS...

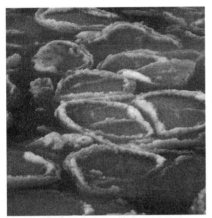

This frozen patch may affect oceans around the globe.

Ice now covers the area of the Greenland Sea where the Odden Feature should appear—a "natural pump" which helps control the circulation of the world's oceans. It has formed every year in living memory, but began to falter in 1972. It completely failed in 1994, and has not formed since. The possible effect on the world's oceans is not known.

WHEN IT RAINS...

Spain's drought was resolved in the spring, although probably not in the way the Spanish would have preferred. Torrential winter rains not only refilled reservoirs which had been lying half empty, but caused catastrophic floods in some areas. Seville's schools were closed; dams burst; farms became unworkable; crops were ruined. Some areas which had imposed water rationing now have enough in reserve for the next three years.

STILL HOTTER

The World Meteorological Organization has issued a statement that the world is officially hotter. Echoing an earlier warning from the Meteorological Office in Britain, they said that worldwide temperatures for 1995 were, on average, 0.72° higher than any year in the last three decades. Parts of Siberia were 5.4° hotter. They also noted that 1995 had 19 tropical storms in the Atlantic, of which 11 reached hurricane strength or higher—the second highest total since records began in 1886. The report also said that depletion of the ozone layer started earlier in the year and lasted longer than before. The ozone hole was measured at 8.8 million square miles, just short of its 1993 peak.

THE BIG CHILL

The United States suffered a "cold wave" to match last year's heatwave. Over 60 people are believed to have died as a result of the record low temperatures, including one unfortunate elderly Chicagoan who managed to survive the city's apocalyptic heat in the summer of 1995, only to freeze to death in her apartment on February 1. Temperatures as low as –51°F were recorded. After the chill came the thaw, and the inevitable floodwater. The Pacific Northwest was particularly badly hit, with the worst flooding of Oregon and Washington rivers in thirty years, causing thousands to evacuate their homes.

FERTILITY SEATS

❦ The Birkat Yosef supermarket in Ashod, Israel, was opened in 1992 to provide cheap food for the poor, but soon found itself providing a less orthodox service. The first cashier to use the chair by the cash register—one Orly Revivo—went to her doctor after several weeks of nausea, and was told she was pregnant. The supermarket's owner, Victor Vaknin, replaced her with a woman called Tami, who only lasted a couple of weeks before discovering that she, too, was pregnant. Her replacement was Vaknin's wife, who soon became pregnant with her ninth child. Another store worker, Ester Dahan, was unwittingly tricked into the chair by friends; one month later, she was pregnant.

Orly Revivo, who had originally refused to use the chair for fear of becoming pregnant a second time, was sent to work at the checkout again; she duly became pregnant, a mere three months after the birth of her first child. At this point, the chair's fame began to spread. Ten assistants in all had become pregnant after sitting in it, and they seem to have told a lot of people. The chair eventually had to be housed on its own in the store's bomb shelter. During this time, it was credited with a further 25 births; apparently even sterile men reported benefits from sitting in it.

Sadly, it seems that there was too much sitting and not enough shopping. The supermarket had to close recently—our sources are vague about exactly when—and its entire stock was seized by the city council in lieu of some 400,000 shekels (about $135,000) in debts. According to Mr. Vaknin, a group of "important rabbis" were to decide what should be done with the chair; sadly, news of their decision has yet to reach us.

❦ In the summer of 1995, an Asda supermarket in Llandudno, England, had three contemporaneous pregnancies, all attributed to an office chair in the reception area. The three women involved—Mair Roberts, Margaret Hughes and Mary Jones—are apparently the third group of women at the store to simultaneously discover that they were pregnant. The store's Deputy Customer Services Manager, Janine Parkynn, explained, "[The three women] have all become pregnant and are all due in November. Previously, three female staff got pregnant within one month of one another and had their babies. They came back to work and the same thing happened again. It was exactly the same office and exactly same job." Other female staff, including Ms. Parkynn, were reportedly now wary of sitting in the chair.

❦ In January, another Asda market, this one in Kendal, England, mustered an impressive total of 13 pregnancies among the women who had staffed a particular checkout. According to Customer Service Manager Sheila Hindon: "We began to take notice when the sixth woman became pregnant. We thought it was a freak coincidence, but it became a bit of a joke when, one after the other, 13 women announced the news." The husbands of four of the cashiers have, reportedly, banned their wives from working at register number 11, which Asda has temporarily renamed register 10a.

COSMOLOGICAL SUPERLATIVES

RINGS AROUND THE SUN

A rainbow ring around the Sun, called a corona, was spotted over Dorchester Heights in Massachusetts on June 29, 1995. While coronas are often sighted around the Moon, it's rare to catch a glimpse of the celestial circle during day. A similar solar halo was seen across Sussex, England, on May 1. Matt Arris, forecaster at Southampton Weather Centre, explained that such halos occur when there is a very thin sheet of ice crystals in high cloud, at a specific angle to the Sun's rays.

ONE-MAN-BAND PULSAR

NASA scientists are still puzzled as to the precise nature of GROJ1744–28, a new astronomical object discovered recently in the direction of our galactic center, writes Paul Parsons.

The object, which was first observed by NASA's Burst and Transient Source Experiment (BATSE), sporadically radiates X rays with a luminosity close to one million times that generated by our sun. While being the most active source of X-ray and gamma-ray bursts in the sky, it also emits additional radiation in periodic flashes. It is this latter behavior that has led to it being classified as a pulsar.

Pulsars are like cosmic lighthouses, characterized by their regular electromagnetic emissions. These pulses are sent out at intervals of a few seconds or less. Structurally, they comprise a rapidly rotating neutron star—a body with approximately the mass of the Sun and with a diameter of the order of six miles—that emits radiation in two diametrically opposed beams as the star revolves.

The object is also in a 12-day binary orbit around a low-mass partner and, in addition to X-ray and gamma-ray emissions, faint visible and radio sources have also been resolved in the direction from which the X rays are emanating. "We've seen some sources that play the drums, some that crash cymbals and a few that play the trumpet, but this source is a one-man band," said Fred Lamb, an astrophysicist at the University of Illinois.

Astronomers at NASA are working against the clock to find a complete theoretical model that will explain the behavior of this bursting pulsar which, due to its extreme luminosity, is expected to fade below the limits of detection within the next few months.

COMET HYAKUTAKE X RAYS BAFFLE SCIENTISTS

Comet Hyakutake developed a bizarre, crescent-shaped, X-ray glow extending some 30,000 miles on April 4. It's the first time X rays have ever been detected coming from a comet and scientists are at a loss to explain the observation.

The comet, officially known as C/1996 b2, was named after Yuji Hyakutake, the Japanese amateur astronomer who discovered it through his binoculars on January 30. At that time, it was still beyond the orbit of Mars. By late March, it was visible to the naked eye, the brightest comet since Comet West in 1976. The last time Hyakutake came our way was somewhere between 9,000 and 15,000 years ago. It is the brightest comet to come this close to Earth since 1556.

The comet made its closest approach to Earth on March 25, when it was some 9.3 million miles away, about one-tenth the distance between Earth and the Sun. Two days later, there were signs that one or more chunks had broken loose from its nucleus.

On April 3, sky watchers had the added pleasure of a total lunar eclipse, showing our old neighbor clearly as a sphere rather than a disc.

GALILEO AT GANYMEDE

On June 27, NASA's Galileo probe delivered some of the most spectacular images to date of Jupiter's moon, Ganymede. Ganymede is one of the four largest moons orbiting Jupiter. Passing within 519 miles of it, the satellite has made some startling discoveries.

The observations reveal the presence of intense volcanic and tectonic phenomena on the surface. Many regions of the pocked and cratered surface are situated next to flat, featureless areas, indicating that the cratering has been smoothed away by magma flows, brought to the moon's surface during seismic activity and volcanic eruptions. "These images reveal fundamental details about how features seen by Voyager formed and show us age relationships and sequences that turn our previous thinking upside down," commented one member of the imaging team for the probe.

Ganymede was also found to have its own magnetosphere, a region of charged particles surrounding it and held in place by a strong magnetic field. The presence of the magnetic field suggests either that the moon has a molten iron core, or that it has currents of conducting salt water circulating beneath its icy surface. This is the first time a moon has been found to possess its own magnetic field. Embedded within Jupiter's own magnetic field, it creates a unique "magnetosphere within a magnetosphere."

Chances of Ganymede playing host to indigenous life are slim, as its equatorial temperature can fall below -240°. During the next two years, there are to be three more close flybys of Ganymede, as well as detailed surveys of the three other Galilean moons, Io, Callisto and Europa.

ARIES TO BLAME FOR RAMS ON THE ROAD

Drivers born under the sign of Aries, the ram live up to their name by being more likely to have accidents than those born under other signs of the zodiac, according to research conducted by the Bournemouth, England–based Zurich Municipal Insurance Company. Aries are also more likely to pass on the right or run a red light. However, the company has no intention of charging higher premiums to Arien policy holders.

According to psychologist Susan Blackmore, climate rather than the stars is probably responsible for some typical characteristics. Babies born in the spring under the sign of Aries, for instance, are more likely to be left out in their baby carriages to enjoy the fresh air. In later years this could perhaps lead to a fondness for open-topped sports cars—which are involved in more accidents than family wagons.

This hardly sounds more convincing than the astrological argument.

Zurich's rankings of star signs, from highest number of insurance claims to lowest, is: Aries, Pisces, Virgo, Aquarius, Libra, Gemini, Scorpio, Leo, Taurus, Cancer, Capricorn and Sagittarius.

GEOPHYSICAL ACTIVITY

MOUNTAIN MOURNING

After months of rumbling, Mt. Ruapehu, on New Zealand's North Island, erupted in mid-June, blasting lava and hot ash into the night sky, followed by a scientific assurance that volcanic activity was subsiding. Local authorities imposed an exclusion zone around the volcano; airports were closed and planes rerouted mid-flight. Maori folklore has it that Mt. Ruapehu is the bride of the dormant Mt. Taranaki, and is weeping for its husband.

RUNNING LATE

The famous Old Faithful geyser in Wyoming's Yellowstone National Park appears not to be quite as faithful as it once was. It gained its nickname on account of its uncannily regular eruptions; at the turn of the century, it was touted as spouting "every hour on the hour." However, the interval between eruptions has been getting longer and more irregular in recent years. In 1950, it was 62 minutes; in 1970, 66 minutes. Now eruptions are 77 minutes apart, give or take ten minutes. Park rangers are blaming earthquakes for disturbing the spout's schedule.

NOT-SO-SOLID GROUND

A three-story Tudor house in San Francisco collapsed into a sinkhole in December 1995. The hole, in Seacliff, was believed to have been caused by heavy rain, which ruptured a 100-year-old sewer. As well as the house, the hole claimed a tree, a truck, part of a neighboring house and some power lines. The hole was 200 feet wide and 60 feet deep.

MYSTERY HOLES IN FROZEN LAKE

At the end of 1995, Mats Andersson saw smoke moving over the surface of Glasshult Lake in Torup, Sweden. Later he found holes in the ice covering the lake, which had not frozen over, despite it being 20 degrees below freezing. The holes were star-shaped and about ten feet apart. The snow was slushy and wet in a circle of about a 65-foot radius surrounding the holes. It was as if something was heating the water from underneath the ice. The Civil Aviation Authority denied that any plane had lost parts over the lake; and the astronomical observatory at Uppsala thought it almost impossible that several meteorites could have fallen in the same lake.

IT'S A YAM'S WORLD

Farmer Vo Nhu Da from central Vietnam discovered a man-sized sweet potato weighing 187 pounds on January 27. News of the find spread fast and before long he was inundated with throngs of curious visitors. To escape them, he locked himself in his house with the potato. He then sold the prodigious vegetable to a hotel owner, who charged visitors a dime a glimpse.

RANGOON RUBY

A flawless, nine-and-a-half-pound ruby, said to be the world's largest, has been discovered in Burma. The 21,450-carat stone, about five inches by seven inches, was found in Mogok, 435 miles north of Rangoon. It easily beats the largest ruby listed by Guinness (8,500 carat). It will be displayed uncut at the state gem museum.

MUCH TOO MUSH

Three giant mushrooms sprouted in Suphanburi Province, home of the Thai prime minister, Banharn Silpa-archa. Each was 14 inches tall and 16–19 inches across the cap, and the trio was nicknamed "gold," "copper" and "money" by locals. People came from all over the province to offer prayers and incense before the mushrooms. Thais believe that rare things might herald good luck, particularly in the lottery.

DUNE CROON

A series of singing dunes has been discovered in the Badainjaran Desert in Inner Mongolia. Researchers from the Chinese Academy of Science found that the dunes sing or groan when a soft wind blows over them, making the sound of an airplane in flight. The sound is caused when grains of uniform size rub against each other.

THE
PARANORMAL
WORLD

THE PARANORMAL WORLD

This is the true essence of Forteana—the data that boggles, stymies, inspires and outrages. These are the events, activities, and experiences that just don't jibe with current scientific theories of the universe.

UFOs dominated the Paranormal World last year. Sightings were reported from all over the world; an insurance company attempted to claim that they had incontrovertible proof of Alien Abductions; *Independence Day* prompted a wave of media interest in UFOs. Miracles were slightly down on the previous year's crop, but Images were up, with a spontaneous image of the Virgin Mary appearing on an American office building and a cinnamon danish which bore an uncanny resemblance to Mother Teresa.

PSYCHICAL PHENOMENA

CYBERSPOONS

Stress his spoon and win $1 million.

Uri Geller announced his latest challenge to the world's psychokinetics—bend a spoon over the Internet and win $1 million. This is believed to be the first attempt to test whether psychic powers can be made to work over the Infobahn.

Geller's challenge uses a "live" Internet video image of a spoon inside a see-through safe in his Berkshire,

England, home. Would-be spoon-benders should point their browsers at "Uri Geller's Psychic City" (http://www.urigeller.com) and concentrate on bending the spoon; stress gauges on the spoon will register any movement of more than 5 degrees. If the spoon bends, anyone who is logged on at the time will be invited to put on a repeat performance in front of Geller himself and David Berglas, president of Magic Circle, along with representatives of Broadsystem, the event's sponsors, and Cornhill, who have insured the spoon for $1 million against being bent.

The whole experiment will be monitored by Stephen Ross and David Robertson from the University of London, who have published several papers on psychic phenomena. Their methods will be based on those of Professor John Hasted, who conducted research into Geller's powers in the 1970s.

The challenge was announced—for mystical reasons that were never made entirely clear—at 11:11 a.m. on January 11 (1/11). Geller spoke at length about his own successes in psi experimentation, including the claim that it was he who had begun the CIA's psi experiments, in 1973. He also suggested that the challenge's ultimate winner will come from Japan.

Other attractions on Uri's web page include a plug for his business consulting services, some biographical details, and a plug for the Geller biopic *Mindbender*. Budding psychics can practice their skills for the $1 million challenge by playing an interactive dowsing game called Strike!

PECULIAR PRESS

UNICORN SAFE THANKS TO CASH
The Stage, September 14, 1995

**MYTHICAL BEAST BRINGS
CITY GRIM MESSAGE**
Southampton Daily Echo,
September 5, 1995

500 ELVES LOOSE
Daily Echo, December 15,
1994

He has also entered into a rather unlikely arrangement with a leading British fashion house. Legendary Manchester fashion label Joe Bloggs has teamed up with Geller to produce the world's first psychic line of clothing. Each item will be touched by Geller before it arrives in the shops. On the first day of each month, Geller will "focus his powers and visualize the public wearing the line," sending out "positive energy" to the wearers.

Geller will be donating a "considerable" percentage of his profits to Save the Children.

STRANGE DEATHS

❦ Andrea Ruga, 47, had the same name, birthplace and date of birth as a Mafia godfather accused of terrorism and kidnapping. Italy's police computers couldn't tell them apart and the "impeccably honest" ironmonger from Monasterace in southern Italy constantly had his house raided. At roadblocks his wife and children sat weeping as he was hustled off to have his papers checked. At hotels he suffered countless indignities as staff called the police.

On October 24, 1995, he was found dead after taking poison. Minutes before, he had phoned three senators, three magistrates, a newspaper editor and the local police chief to say that he couldn't stand the aggravation anymore.

❦ Two wedding guests died in a gun battle in Aswan, Egypt, after the bride offended family honor by holding her husband's hand, breaking an ancient custom of not showing affection in public.

❦ According to France's veterans affairs minister, several World War I veterans died of joy after hearing they were to receive the Legion of Honor to mark the 77th anniversary of the war's end. He said he knew of at least two who died filling in the form to receive the award.

❦ Edward Musgrove, 32, attacked his estranged wife as she began an evening route as a Los Angeles bus driver. He grabbed the steering wheel, causing the bus to veer off the road, hit a tree and crash into a brick wall. The woman was not injured, but Musgrove was hurled through the windshield into the wall and decapitated.

❦ An aphrodisiac called "Rock Hard," thought to have been imported from Hong Kong, killed four New York men over two years when they swallowed it instead of rubbing it on their genitals. The Food and Drug Administration blamed the deaths on poor labeling.

TWINED TWINS

As is so often the case with identical twins, William (Bill) and John Bloomfield, 61, shared everything throughout their lives, even illnesses and operations.

They grew up in Hobart, Tasmania, where they worked in a shoe store called Bloomfields, run by their mother, and moved to Perth, Australia, in 1989. They lived together, sharing a double bed, and were believed to be gay. They often strolled around the Perth suburb of Victoria Park and usually dressed in identical oriental clothing, both sporting gypsy earrings. According to neighbor Ashley Williams, "their foot and arm actions were the same, like it was one person walking." They were involved in the Sai Baba cult (among others). They had hip replacement operations in the same hospital at the same time. They entertained regularly in their younger years, but then became more reclusive.

On May 27, Bill and John went to Perth's Burswood Casino to watch a body-building contest. Near midnight, Bill went to the restaurant, his brother intending to join him in a few minutes. Bill suddenly collapsed and died from a suspected heart attack. An emergency call for an ambulance was logged at 12:14 a.m. At 12:16 a.m. another call came from the casino; John Bloomfield had also keeled over. The twin brothers' lives ended within a mere two minutes of each other.

The coroner's office had a real problem identifying which brother was which: apart from dressing identically, they had the same scars and freckles in identical places. Each had short-cropped grey hair, wore spectacles with neck cords and carried canes. They were more like clones than twins. Dental records might be the only way to identify which twin was which.

There was another pair of identical twins living in Perth, called Bill and John Bromfield, whose family received misguided messages of condolence; but the Bromfield twins are 53 and in good health. They are both married and live separately; both work in separate dairies, although they do the same job. Bill's wife, Muriel, said that some extraordinary things had happened, such as the twins independently buying the same shoes from the same shop on the same day. "When Bill injured his shoulder in a motorcycle accident," she said, "John phoned and asked, 'Is Bill alright? I've got this terrible pain in my shoulder.'"

MIND OVER MATTER

According to a New Scientist report, research at the University of California at Berkeley indicates that it may be possible for people to influence events that have already taken place.

Henry Stapp of UCB has been working on an explanation for the results of a set of highly controversial experiments carried out by paranormal investigator Henry Schmidt in San Antonio, Texas. In Schmidt's experiments, a radioactive decay counter was used to generate a random sequence of positive and negative numbers. The sequence was revealed to no one. Some months later, a group of martial arts students, trained in concentration, were the first to see the sequence—one number at a time. The students were asked to mentally influence the sequence in favor of positive numbers.

Strangely, they seem to have man-

CLAIRVOYANT FORESAW OWN DEATH

❦ Vangelia Gushterova, a blind, web-fingered peasant clairvoyant vener-ated throughout Bulgaria as "Aunt" or "Granny" Vanga, died of cancer in a Sofia hospital aged 85 on August 11. Born in neighboring Macedonia in 1911, Vanga found fame after losing her sight at the age of 12 during a windstorm. Later, she was able to help locate missing relatives and people who had been kidnapped.

Most of her predictions related to people's private lives, but she was said to have foreseen World War II, the coming to power of the Com-munists in 1944, the invasion of Czechoslovakia in 1968 and an earth-quake in northern Bulgaria in 1985. More than a million people sought guidance from the seer, including respected intellectuals and notable politicians. Her advice was usually uttered in a trance. She was con-sulted regularly by the Communist dictator Todor Zhivkov and at vari-ous times by Leonid Brezhnev, Mikhail Gorbachev and Vladimir Zhiri-novsky. She is said to have foretold the time of her own death.

Vanga claimed to derive her power from an ancient city buried under Rupite, her village 100 miles south of Sofia near the Greek border. Boil-ing water bubbles from the earth outside her house, and many believe it has curative power. Waves of colored light were sometimes seen in the sky above her house. The current president and prime minister and tens of thousands of ordinary Bulgarians attended her funeral.

aged it. The pre-recorded sequence had a significant bias toward positive numbers in the sequence, one which had less than 1 in 1000 probability of appearing at random.

Attempting an explanation, Stapp cites the part of quantum theory that says that observation of an event alters the nature of that event. The late Eu-gene Wigner held that consciousness was fundamentally involved in the nature of quantum events—that an atom only decays (or fails to decay) when it is observed to do so, and that it exists in an indeterminate state un-til it is observed. Thus, according to Stapp, the outcome of the radioactive decay in Schmidt's experiments did not become fixed until the number sequences were displayed to the mar-tial artists. However, this does not fully display the bias of the numbers.

In order to account for this, Stapp introduces a concept of "non-linear-ity," which suggests that the observer's brain is part of a quantum system along with, for example, the numbers in Schmidt's sequences as they were displayed. Since the results are theo-retically indeterminate until ob-served, the implication seems to be that the observer's brain can actually exert influence on the events which it observes, as long as the outcome of the events is indeterminate.

The implications of this haven't yet been fully worked out, although Stapp feels that his theories preserve the causality which is apparently vio-lated by Schmidt's findings. However, other physicists feel that Stapp is vio-lating the law of physics that prevents the travel of information at speeds faster than light.

PROPHECIES

ANTICHRISTMAS

In the days leading up to June 6, 1996, the sixth day of the sixth month in a year ending in six, a pamphlet warned the people of Bogota, Colombia, that the Antichrist (whose number is 666) would claim their unbaptized children on that dread day. Although the prediction was made by a Protestant fundamentalist group, many Roman Catholics picked up on the rumor, panicked and rushed to have their children baptized. About 20,000 people were baptized in the city over the weekend of June 1–2, ten times the average. The emergency baptisms were televised, which led to hysteria spreading across the country.

The rumor took several forms. In one, the Antichrist's birth was expected, a prediction that terrified pregnant women due to give birth in early June. In another, an evil being was expected to possess any unbaptized children and mark them with the Sign of the Beast. And in yet another rumor, closely allied to the familiar folklore tale of kidnapping for the organ trade, it was feared that the Antichrist would steal children from their parents.

KILLER MAMMARIES DOOMED TO DROP

All five members of Brazil's hottest rock band died last March when their plane crashed into a hill above Guarulhos, their hometown, near Sao Paulo's airport. The Mamonas Assassinas (Killer Mammaries) were returning from the final concert of a five-month tour. Last December, Sao Paulo soothsayer Mother Dinah predicted in the daily Folha da Tarde that they would be involved in a plane crash. Hours before the last concert, hair salon owner Nélson de Lima videotaped keyboard player Júlio Rasec as he was having his hair dyed red. "Last night I dreamed something," said a concerned Júlio on the tape. "It seemed the airplane was falling."

As they boarded the plane that night in Brasilia for the flight to Guarulhos, a runway worker wished them luck in their forthcoming overseas debut: "I hope you're a smash in Portugal." Replied lead singer Dinho Alves: "It's my head I'm going to smash."

SCALES OF FATE

Four baby albino crocodiles were recently bought for $9,000 by a hotelier in Phnom Penh, Cambodia. The white crocodile is a most auspicious symbol in Khmer folklore and is said to appear only when the country is at a crossroads. Shortly after one was spotted in the Mekong River in 1970, Prince Norodom Sihanouk was overthrown in a coup.

QABBALAH CURSE CLUE TO RABIN MURDER

The November 4, 1995, shooting of Yitzhak Rabin, Israel's prime minister and architect of its peace initiatives, shocked the world but did not come as a surprise to at least one extreme religious group. The assassination was predicted in an issue of the *Jerusalem*

Report, a prominent Israeli biweekly magazine (which, although dated November 16, was actually published in the week before the event). In an article by Peter Hirschberg, it is revealed that an unnamed rabbi, immersed in study of the Qabbalah—an ancient tradition of Jewish mysticism—had placed a devastating curse on the premier on October 3, the eve of Yom Kippur, held to be a magically efficacious date.

The rabbi, who would only identify himself as a member of the ultra-right Kach movement inspired by the late Meir Kahane, said confidently that the effects of the curse would not be immediate but would become apparent within 30 days. One day off is not bad prophecy (although Rabin might dispute this).

Over in New York, Rabbi Jacob Bronner, a former adviser to former mayor Koch, offered this prosaic assessment of the curse: "Every week, people were saying he was going to die. If all of a sudden, he was walking down the street and a lightning bolt hit him, I'd have second thoughts . . . but someone got a gun and shot him. Give me a break!"

Our correspondent Mike Crowley reminded us: "Other victims of qabbalistic curses in modern times include Gershon Avron, the mayor of Jerusalem in the 1950s who introduced the first mixed-sex swimming pool [and died of hepatitis], and Eyal Ragonis, chairman of a construction company that built a bank over an ancient cemetery [and died of a heart attack]."Curiously, these curses seem effective only against fellow Jews as, during the Gulf War, equally elaborate ritual cursing of Saddam Hussein, demanding not just his death but that his widow be given to another man, has yet to be fulfilled.

DOTH THE VATICAN PROTEST TOO MUCH?

The Vatican has warned the faithful about the activity of a Greek Orthodox "medium" in Switzerland who is announcing messages said to be celestial revelations. The Congregation for the Doctrine of the Faith (i.e. the Inquisition) has ordered Catholics not to accept her writings. One can only wonder why this soothsayer has provoked such a strong reaction.

DIAMOND DISCOVERIES

❖ Liliana Parodi did not have to pay for her pasta in her favorite restaurant in Genoa, Italy, after a small stone wedged in one of her teeth. The next day the stone was removed and turned out to be an uncut diamond worth nearly $3,200.

❖ Five-year-old Nicole Ohlsen of Bochum in Germany found a doll on a trash heap. When she took it home, her mother nearly threw it out before discovering a cache of diamonds inside—$72,000 worth. Police told the family they can keep the gems, which will be used to pay for Nicole's education.

❖ Surgeons operating on 67-year-old Janet Webb's "tumor" in Cedar Rapids, Iowa, found a diamond ring, lost 44 years earlier during a caesarean operation. The same thing happened to Virginia Argue in Roseville, California, six months earlier. She had carried a diamond ring in her stomach for 50 years.

APPARITIONS

LEGLESS GHOST HAS BOSNIANS SPOOKED IN TUZLA BOMBSITE

The mortar shells have stopped falling in Bosnia, but still no one drives by Kapija Square in Tuzla's old town after midnight. The square has been deserted since word spread that the ghost of one of the 71 young people killed in a Bosnian Serb mortar attack on May 25, 1995, had been seen at the blast site, searching in vain for her severed legs.

The ghost was spotted last December by a military police officer, Mustafa Piric, who had stopped a girl with long, blond hair after curfew to ask for her identification papers. When she turned around, he saw that she had no face, and then he heard her cry: "Give me back my legs!"

"A lot of people here believe in ghosts and spirits," said Alma Ahmedbegovic, a 20-year-old radio reporter who helped pull dying friends from the rubble in the square. "They believe this girl's spirit can't rest because she was buried without her legs."

The mass funeral for the victims was held secretly in the middle of the night for fear of another attack. A flower-covered memorial has been erected; the incident had great emotional impact on the town, as virtually everyone knew someone who had been killed. Many have awoken from nightmares to see their dead friends standing before them as if they were real.

SPOOKED!

❧ Mary Johnson and fellow actor Robert LeBrecht were lurking in the shadows to scare tourists on an Isle of Wight, England, ghost walk when they heard footsteps crunching on the gravel behind them, but there was nobody in sight. They were at a famous local haunt in Newport where a monk was murdered, and Ms. Johnson suggested the monk's ghost was annoyed because she was dressed as a friar.

❧ Sightings of a spectral young woman with fair hair, dressed in modern casual clothes, have been unnerving early morning cleaners at Bo'ness Academy, West Lothian, Scotland. One of the women, Mary Cunningham, said: "I felt someone behind me and turned and saw her. She reached out to touch me and when I let out a squeal she just disappeared. I felt sick with fear and was off work for a couple of days." Workmate Maisie King, 62, also saw the ghost and their supervisor, Diane Prow, had "felt a presence."

❧ According to Seymour and Neligan's *True Irish Ghost Stories,* Charles Fort, erected in 1667 near Kinsale in Court, is said to be haunted by the White Lady. This ghost has been identified as the daughter of the fort's governor, Colonel Warrender. She died on her wedding day.

IMAGES

SNAPSHOT PICKS UP SHIP'S CREW'S PROP-CHOPPED CHUM

Freddy Jackson appeared in a staff photo taken three days after his death.

The photograph above of the Maintenance Group of HMS Daedalus was taken on the runway at Cranwell in Lincolnshire, England, in 1919. The man half-concealed in the back row, Freddy Jackson, had actually been killed three days earlier. The naval air mechanic died instantly on the same tarmac strip after stumbling into a whirling propeller. Some of those in the official picture to commemorate the disbanding of the transport yard at the base, taken by Bassano's Photographic Company, had marched behind his coffin during the military funeral.

Bobbie Capel, 97, widow of Air Vice Marshal Arthur Capel, was a Wren driver at the base and has no doubt that the face peeping out from the back row is Jackson. She recalls the general astonishment when the photo was pinned up. Her neighbors in the Somerset village of Chipstable recently persuaded her to send the photograph to the *Navy News* with a plea for other witnesses to come forward.

The photo had been mentioned in *Flight Towards Reality* by Air Marshal Sir Victor Goddard, one of the founders of the RAF. "There he was, and no mistake, although a little fainter than the rest," he wrote. "Indeed, he looked as though he was not altogether there; not really with that group, for he alone was capless, smiling; all the rest were serious and set, and wearing service caps. What is somewhat unusual, to say the least, is that this was an official photograph ... also the certainty that there had been no hanky-panky in the darkroom. Not only would Bassano's not have dared to fake it; the negative was scrutinized for faking and was found to be untouched."

Capel said: "I cannot entertain the idea that this was a deliberate fake. For one, the photographer came from outside the base. He didn't know any of us and once he had taken his picture he left immediately. He just would not have known about the accident. I can think of no explanation other than it is the picture of a ghost."

PECULIAR PRESS

THE CORRECT VERSION DECLARES GOD AMBIDEXTROUS
Times, September 1, 1995

ARMAGEDDON COULD THREATEN UNITED'S PROMOTION PUSH
West Cumbria News and Star, January 4, 1995

LORD'S MOTHER SUES DIOCESE
Victoria Times-Colonist, January 21, 1995

THE SCHWASCAR AWARDS

FLYING MANHOLE COVER

❧ Alastair Murray was driving in Aberdeen, Scotland, when a manhole cover shot out of the ground and lifted his Ford Escort about three feet in the air, rupturing its chassis and sending the car 30 feet across the road onto the sidewalk. Police blamed a buildup of air pressure in the sewer after torrential rains, but the water utility said it was a mystery why a heavy lid was thrown up with such force. The answer may have come several months later, when a number of sewage workers were taken ill after breathing a "mystery gas" in the Rosemount area. "We're convinced we're working with gremlins," said a sewage worker.

RUNNERS-UP

❧ Late-night explosions in Delhi's upscale Connaught Place left 14 or 15 people injured and gave 40 manhole covers their first taste of freedom in March 1995. A buildup of methane in the antiquated sewer network was blamed. The explosions were felt over an area of some 1.7 square miles. Some of the injured were thrown 16 feet into the air and the force of the blast cracked large areas of concrete and tarmac. Fires started in several places underground. Another blast hit Connaught Place on November 21, injuring 20 people; whether this was a bomb or more subterranean methane was not stated.

❧ In two other cases, exploding gasoline took the blame. Three drivers in High Wycombe, England, crashed their cars trying to avoid a brace of airborne covers "hurled 200 yards skyward after gasoline from a garage leaked into sewers and exploded." In Australia, a number of covers went up near Brisbane. It was believed that vandals had poured gasoline down a storm drain on the Nerang-Southport road and threw lighted matches. In neither case did anyone actually produce evidence that these explosions, or the subsequent fire in the sewers in Brisbane, were caused by gasoline.

❧ After a 1993 spate of exploding manhole covers and sewage fountains in North Liverpool, England, the city council called in hydraulics expert Dr. Rafid Al-Khaddar, who discovered that there was not enough ventilation in the drainage system. During heavy rain, air was pushed upward, forcing the manhole covers to be fired as if from a cannon. One lid launched itself with such force that it took a substantial portion of the surrounding road with it. A special type of water seal was devised, which allowed the buildup of air to escape while keeping foul smells in their proper place.

SPECTER SHOT IN THE FLAMES

The photograph at right was taken by amateur photographer Tony O'Rahilly at the height of the fierce blaze which destroyed the town hall in Wem, England, in November 1995. It was taken from the road with a 200 mm lens and seems to show a girl standing in the doorway of the town hall's fire escape leading to Noble Street. O'Rahilly said he didn't see the figure until the film was developed on March 4 this year. It has been suggested that the figure is the ghost of the girl who started the Great Fire of Wem which virtually destroyed the small market town in 1677.

Tony Adams, chief photographer at the *Shropshire Star,* has examined the strip of negatives including the picture reproduced here and found no evidence of tampering. Before the photograph was developed, terrified workmen refurbishing the town hall reported seeing a ghostly figure emerge in a swirl of mist, and the town councilors were considering calling in paranormal investigators.

An apparition of a young girl is seen in this photograph of a flaming town hall.

BAD LUCK

BALLBUSTER

A man staggered into the emergency room of Belfast Hospital, Northern Ireland, with a wind-up turtle attached to his testicles. He explained to medical staff that his young son had dropped the toy into his bath. "A mechanical joint connected to his tender bits and jammed solid," said a nurse.

AROUND THE WORLD IN A DAZE

Truck driver Stephen Rees, 36, from Great Horton, England, flew to the Philippines to start a new life as a chauffeur. On the way, he stopped off to look at Munich, Madrid, New York, Singapore and Bangkok. On the flight from Thailand to the Philippines, he fell asleep and missed the stopover in Manila. When he awoke, the plane was approaching Tokyo. He telephoned his new employer to be told he had lost the job. He had only $80 and the clothes he was wearing, since his suitcase had been taken off in Manila.

The British consul was unable to help. Rees spent the night in the airport until he was befriended by three Canadian construction workers who gave him work to raise money for his flight home. He flew to Seoul, South Korea, thinking this would be the easiest route back to England, but as he had no visa he was deported to Hong Kong. Officials in Hong Kong sent him straight back to Seoul. He fought with South Korean immigration officials, and Korean Air agreed to fly him home. Before leaving, he telephoned a friend in Bradford to pick him up at Heathrow.

When he arrived in England some 17 days after he had set out, immigration officials didn't believe that he was the same man as the smart person in his passport photograph. Special Branch held him for several hours on suspicion of being an illegal immigrant and, by the time he had convinced them of who he was, Rees's friend had assumed that he must have missed the flight and left. After a journey of around 30,000 miles, Mr. Rees hitchhiked home.

WIN SOME, LOSE SOME

Since winning $16.2 million in the Pennsylvania State Lottery in 1988, Buddy Post's life has been "a nightmare." In 1991, he was sentenced to two years' imprisonment for assaulting his stepdaughter's boyfriend in a business argument. In 1992 he was ordered to give one-third of the jackpot to his former landlady, Ann Karpik, who claimed she shared the ticket with him.

In 1993, his brother Jeffrey was convicted of plotting to kill him and his wife to get the money. Then his sixth wife, Constance, whom he had married after his win, upped and left him.

He has spent so much on litigation that he has been declared bankrupt with debts of $500,000 even though he has yet to collect almost $5 million of his winnings. The gas company cut supplies to the crumbling mansion he bought, and his bar—along with other business ventures—went bust.

Now Mr. Post, a 58-year-old former carnival worker and cook who lives in Oil City, wants to sell the 17 installments of the lottery win due to him for $2.15 million—half their value. Lottery officials are threatening legal action to stop him. He reckons that if he can sell the remaining winnings, he can clear his debts, buy his house and still have $700,000 left over.

Mr. Post, who has sold the film rights to his life story, plans to pursue lawsuits he has filed against police, judges and lawyers who he says conspired to take his money.

FALLING PRAY

Worshipers who gathered to pray for protection on July 15, an astrologically unlucky day, were trapped in stampedes at two Hindu shrines. A total of 58 people died, some crushed and others impaled on a bamboo barricade. In Haridwar on the Ganges, at least 21 were killed when pilgrims stampeded over a narrow bridge near a Shiva temple.

OUT OF THE FRYING PAN AND INTO THE FIRE

A family found themselves trapped between flames and fangs during a day trip to Woburn Safari Park. Steven and Jane Marshall from Cambridgeshire, England, took their two children and Mrs. Marshall's mother, Doris, for a day trip to the safari park in Bedfordshire on August 7.

While they were in the tiger reserve, smoke started pouring from the engine of their Renault Espace. Rangers positioned Land Rovers on either side of the Renault to protect the trapped Marshalls from the nine tigers; the rescue was just in time, as the Espace's engine caught fire mo-

ments after the family escaped it.

•The Marshalls' ordeal was a rerun of that suffered by Malcom and Sue Burt, whose Renault 25 caught fire in the tiger enclosure at Longleat on August 10, 1994. The Burts were unable to open the windows or doors because the electronic locking system had shorted out in the fire; warden John Mizen managed to frighten away the tigers just as the Burts forced open the driver's door and leapt into his patrol car.

FLESHBOMBS!

❦ The fate of Les Kupi seems like revenge for the dynamiting of a whale on an Oregon beach. Mr. Kupi was among a crowd gathering around a dead whale that had beached on the shore of Northumberland Strait, near Marshville, Nova Scotia. He noticed a trickle of blood from the whale's mouth and bent for a closer look. Without warning, a loud groan issued from deep inside the creature and a flood of blood and "other matter" drenched him. "It was disgusting," said Mr. Kupi.

❦ Horrible, in a different way, was the scene in a mortuary chapel at Bacau, Romania. When a family paid their respects to their dead elderly relative, the body exploded. "It was like something from a horror movie," said one shocked relative. The family were too poor to have the body embalmed and blamed two days of hot weather.

GOOD LUCK

CHEESY LANDING

The pilot of a light plane and his passenger claimed to have escaped unhurt after stuffing their cargo of soft cheese into the cockpit to absorb the impact when their plane crash-landed in Wisconsin. Passenger Frank Emmert, 36, said: "We were smelly but alive."

FIRST ALERT

On November 2, 1995, in Wolverhampton, England, fire broke out in a home's bathroom exhaust fan. Heat from the fire burned through the fan's plastic casing, causing the motor to fall out and hit an aerosol can of shaving cream. The can exploded, sprayed foam everywhere and extinguished the fire. Homeowner Jeff Crooks slept right through the crisis.

GOLDEN HANDSHAKE

While emptying his desk on the day he was fired, Munich office worker Frederick Baum found a prepaid coupon for soccer match betting. He filled it in and won $640,000.

DIGITAL DISCOVERY

An eight-fingered Sydney man was finally reunited with his two wayward digits 25 years after losing them in an accident with a circular saw. The mummified fingers were discovered in a pile of wallpaper by workers demolishing a house.

SAVED BY THE BELL

Fahed Subitan, an Arab worker at Israel's only crocodile farm, in the Jordan Valley, tripped over a coil of hosepipe as he fled from a 12-foot female crocodile, possibly angry as it was the laying season. He lay sprawled on the ground expecting the worst when there was a ringing sound. His mobile phone had fallen out of his pocket as he hit the ground, and his girlfriend had chosen that moment to put in a call. The beast paused, looked at Subitan, looked at the telephone ... and swallowed it. Its hunger seemingly satisfied, it then disappeared back into its pool. Giora Garber, manager of the crocodile farm, said: "Afterwards we rang the mobile number. All we got was the busy signal." Naturally, everyone recalled the crocodile in *Peter Pan* which swallowed an alarm clock, not to mention Captain Hook's hand.

SPLAT MARKS THE SPOT

Charlotte Muse remembers the day she and her co-workers were chasing a fly around the office, failing in their attempts to swat it with rolled-up magazines. The fly landed in a heavy book and someone slammed it shut. The book was a dictionary and the ill-fated insect had been smashed against the word "housefly."

Musing on Ms. Muse's letter, columnist Leah Garchik explained why it had won her "coincidence grand prize": "The story was easy to picture; it didn't involve dates, numbers or brothers-in-law; and no one sent in anything like it."

SIBLING SERENDIPITY

❤ Student Tim Henderson, 29, hitched a ride to London with diving engineer Mark Knight, 31, because he couldn't afford the train fare from Newcastle. The pair had been matched up by the Freewheelers Lift Share Agency on Tyneside, which had 16,000 names on its register. They started talking about friends and relatives. "There was a moment of complete silence as we both stared at each other in disbelief," said Mr. Henderson. "Then one of us said: 'You must be my brother.' It was pretty mind-blowing. I always knew I had a halfbrother but never thought we would meet." Tom Henderson, their father, was divorced from Mark's mother and remarried. Mark's mother remarried and he took his stepfather's last name. Mark and Tim met just once before, when they were five and three, but lost touch due to the family rift. Now they both live in London.

RUNNERS-UP

❤ Lillian Bell, 90, met Fred Marshall, 80, at a retirement home in Ashurst, England. They spent four days exchanging memories of growing up in Yorkshire. Lillian was surprised when Fred's description of his childhood home sounded just like the home she remembered; but it was only when her daughter, Rose Woodfield, came to visit and recognized "Uncle Fred" that the truth dawned—that after 23 years, by pure chance, brother and sister had been reunited. They had both lived in the Tooton area of Southampton when Fred regularly biked over to his sister's for lunch. When the visits stopped, the family believed he had returned to Yorkshire.

❤ Two British sisters separated as babies have been reunited and become next-door neighbors in Australia. Adopted Evelyn Rider was stunned when she discovered that Edna Wilde, her long-lost sister from Castleford, England, had moved into the house next door.

❤ Henry Dawson and Peter Williamson worked alongside each other for seven years in a Milton Keynes, England, factory and often went out together. They then discovered (we are not told how) that they were brothers, separated 40 years ago when one of them was adopted.

❤ Twin sisters who live 400 miles apart sent their mother in Merthyr Tydfil, Wales, identical Christmas cards with the same message.

SECOND WIND

A gust of wind blew Aimé Grosjean, 72, off the balcony of a 17th-floor apartment in Regensdorf, Switzerland. Luckily, another gust of wind blew him onto the balcony of the 16th-floor apartment, the tenants of which were away at the time. The shaken retiree suffered no more than bruises and a cut in his arm.

LUCKY FOR SOME

On July 20, 6,208 players of Connecticut's daily lottery put their money on 8–0–0, the flight number of the TWA jet that crashed into the Atlantic one week before. When the number hit, the lottery had to pay out over $1 million in winnings, about three times what was wagered. The state took in $526,745 on the three-digit game and lost $678,170.

BLIND MAN AT THE WHEEL

José Pinto, who drove to work daily despite being 95 percent blind, was arrested after police received a tip-off from his employer, Spain's National Organization for the Blind. By avoiding shapes and shadows, Mr. Pinto successfully navigated a seven-mile stretch of Madrid traffic for three years. Police stopped him in 1995 for not having a license, but failed to notice his poor vision. Surprisingly, his car didn't have a scratch on it and he was released without charge.

MIRACLES

MILKING IT

September saw a frenzy of activity in the Hindu world, with claims that statues of the god Ganesh were drinking milk. On the 21st, Delhi and much of northern India ran out of milk as rumors spread and the faithful converged on temples to offer their gifts to the gods.

Within hours the rumors had gone worldwide. In Southall, England, a local supermarket reported sales of 25,000 pints in one morning as 10,000 Hindus gathered at the Vishwa temple to feed the god by the spoonful. Apparently the milk vanished from sight as it was supped by the statues, without the stone from which they were made appearing damp or saturated.

Within days, however, the rumors died away with devout Hindus explaining that it was a short-term phenomenon designed by the gods to reassure the faithful of their continuing presence. When a Hindu statue is consecrated, it is believed that the spirit of the god inhabits the material from which it is made.

Milk shortages were reported as the faithful fed the statues.

BLINKING MIRACLE

Car cleaner Layton Brewer, 22, blind in one eye for three years after being struck by a mystery virus, was cured when he accidentally squirted dangerous, caustic cleaning fluid into his eye. "Our only explanation for what's happened is that it's a remarkable coincidence," said a spokesman at Southampton Eye Hospital in England.

•Such short, sharp cures have happened before. A particularly odd (and possibly apocryphal) case was reported in May 1995: blind Indian Gauri Banerjee, 64, knocked his head against a door and regained his sight after 20 years. But in the same moment he lost his hearing.

(UN)LUCKY

A 23-year-old man jumped 220 feet off the San Francisco–Oakland Bay Bridge on December 26, 1995, landing yards from a psychiatrist in a rowboat with a life jacket and a cellular phone. Dennis Tison saw the would-be suicide, tossed him his life jacket and used the phone to call the police.

DAMES AT SEA

In September 1995, two young women were swept off the beach at Brighton, England, by a freak wave and were left clinging to the stilts of the Palace Pier. It was not long before the Brighton coastguard lifeboat turned up—but in attempting to rescue the women the boat crashed into the pier and had itself to be rescued by a lifeboat from Newhaven. The women, it seems, had had an amazing stroke of luck as the Brighton boat had been called out to another distress call and would not have been back in time to save them from the dangerous 12-foot swells. That other call turned out to be a hoax, but placed the boat near the women. Richard Pearce, helmsman of the Brighton lifeboat, said: "Without that hoax call the two women would have been killed."

HOLY FRUITS

Mrs. Ruksana Patel of Daubhill, England, cut open an aubergine in her kitchen and discovered that the seeds spelled out "Ya-Allah" ("Allah exists"). The night before, she had dreamed that one of the three aubergines she had bought was holy and that she would find Allah when she cut it open. Every day, about 50 pilgrims were calling by to witness the miracle. A similar aubergine seed phenomenon attracted 5,000 pilgrims to Leicester in 1990.

Ruksana and her husband Salim, originally from Ahmedabad in Gujarat, India, planned to leave the aubergine on display at their local mosque for a few weeks. Then it would be shared out among the faithful and eaten raw.
•Hindus enjoyed a similar thrill the previous month, when a Ganesh-shaped papaya drew thousands to a Kuala Lumpur temple.

NUTTER SEES VISION OF VIRGIN

In recent months, thousands have flocked to a small Anglican church in Yanaklilla, south of Adelaide, Australia, after Rev. Andrew Nutter described an image of the Virgin Mary and child on the altar wall. "When it first appeared," he said, "I shared it with the congregation and they said: 'Well, yes, if you squint your eyes, maybe. . . .' Now everybody's seeing it."

Nutter first noticed the image in late 1994, but it received little attention outside the parish until the national media got hold of the story after he wrote about it in the local church newspaper in July this year. Nutter said that the vision might have added significance because Yanaklilla was the town where Australia's first prospective saint, the blessed Mary MacKillop, set up the first school of her Sisters of St. Joseph order.

The Anglican diocesan bishop Graham Walden said that the vision did not seem to have been caused by anything such as salt, damp or mold. He pointed out that Anglicans, in contrast to Catholics, did not have any formal process of authentification or proclamation in such a case. "If people receive something as being of God, then it is of God. They don't have some sort of mechanism for accreditation," he said.

MONSTER PYTHON'S HEALING CIRCUS

A Cambodian village has begun worshiping a large python as a god that can heal the sick. According to the Khmer language *Angkor Thom,* the snake was discovered on the night of December 20 under a house in Choeung Tek, a village in the southeastern province of Prey Veng. The houseowner, Neang Tren, planned to take the python to the market for sale the next morning, but his neighbors dreamt of a large snake coming to cure the sick and persuaded him to keep it. The newspaper's front page featured pictures of the saved snake surrounded by adoring villagers, several of whom testified that they had been cured of headaches, dizziness and chest pain after burning incense and laying flowers near the snake. However, some of the faithful were becoming skeptical after a month of snake worship that wasn't paying off.

OFF THE WALL

Rumors that an apparition of Jesus appeared high on a wall on Christmas Day and healed a paralyzed Christian girl drew hundreds of Christians and Muslims to a three-story apartment building in the Iranian capital. On December 27, about 50 people gathered in front of the building on Avanessian Street, situated in an area of East Tehran inhabited mostly by Armenians. They pointed to a mark on the outside wall of the building and insisted that they could see a portrait of Jesus. Someone had spray-painted "Death to rumor-mongers" just below the mark on the wall.

Some of the crowd had other versions of the miracle. One old woman in a black chador said it had happened earlier and it was a Muslim man suffering from cancer who had been healed. She hoped that the miracle could help her husband, who also had cancer. No one answered the bell of the apartment.

POLTERGEISTS

POLTS AND VOLTS

Southern Electricity in England faced a claim that a poltergeist was responsible for Sharon McGrath's $1,350 electricity bill. It had allegedly turned on lights and electrical equipment and shredded telephone directories and bills at her Crowes, Isle of Wight, house.

IN A TIZZY

In the past few months, spectral activity has been noted at the Ilchester Arms in England's Somerset County.

Strange phenomena included the sound of heavy beer barrels being rolled across stone flagstones—even though the flags were removed long ago—and the sound of someone typing close to midnight every evening in a room next to that of barman Wesley Green. After cleaning a bedroom in the empty hotel, a cleaner the next morning was astonished to find that the room had been slept in. The staff said that there was no way that anyone could have gotten in.

"Staff have noticed that glasses have disappeared and suddenly reappeared two days later," said the hotel's

HOT FASHIONS

❧ Chris Williams, a 20-year-old from Port Talbot, England, narrowly escaped injury last February when the shirt he was wearing caught fire. He had bought the $100 Timberland shirt from a Swansea shop called Moustache two months earlier. "We were going out to a family evening and so he decided to wear the shirt," said his mother, Geraldine Williams. "People began commenting on bright lights which appeared on it. A couple of seconds later the front and back burst into flames." Chris was saved from serious injury by a T-shirt he was wearing underneath.

Staff at Moustache immediately removed all their Timberland shirts from sale and offered a refund. "Timberland sent us a letter claiming that the shirt had been subject to a surface flash—suggesting that it had been near a naked flame, which we know wasn't the case," said Mrs. Williams.

❧ Alan Fairless heard a bang in his back garden in Bristol, England, at around 6 a.m. on Sunday, April 21. Unable to figure out what it was, he went back to bed. When he got up some hours later, he discovered that his favorite garment—a green-and-white Lacoste polo shirt pegged on the line to dry—had burned to a crisp, leaving a few bits of green cloth around the shoulders. None of the other items had been affected; checks with the Bristol Weather Centre showed the weather that night had been fine with no lightning in the area. The incident remained a mystery.

owner, Tom Finlay. "A little while ago, 30 glasses vanished and then 26 turned up again. On one occasion we all looked everywhere for a waistcoat that had disappeared. It turned up three days later."

Yeovil medium Flo Essex, a Christian Spiritualist minister, identified the spirit as a mischievous girl called Tizzy, aged 12–14 years who possibly died of rheumatic fever. "Tizzy is very pretty with long hair and blue eyes, a dark dress and white pinafore," said Mrs. Essex. "It was her home and I do not think she has realized she has passed. She is not here to hurt anyone."

"A/C, W/D, LO UTILS, GHOST."

It appears that some inventive realtors are making a resident ghost their unique selling point. Boy's Hall in Kent was offered for sale in 1993 by London estate agency John D. Wood, who made a point of informing prospective buyers of its history of hauntings. The Jacobean hall had been the scene of many gruesome events in its 360-year history; a young Irish dandy was supposedly killed in a secret duel in the grounds after seducing an English officer's wife. Years later another woman's skeleton, dressed in the Irishman's clothes, was found buried under the floor by the lovelorn wife. A woman's ghost has since been seen drifting around the house on "certain nights."

A John D. Wood representative speculated that anyone who tried to sell a house they believed to be haunted without informing the prospective buyer might risk prosecution, as estate agents in the U.K. have to comply with the Property Misdescriptions Act, which sets down strict guidelines for describing a property's particulars. Boy's Hall was eventually sold, for close to the asking price of $1 million.

WINDOW PAINS

Retirees in Riverside Close, England, have been regularly woken by tapping on their windows and ringing on their doorbells; but when they look out nobody is there and no tracks are left in the snow. Police are investigating.

ETERNAL FLAME

For the past three years, Michael Milner has been custodian of the famous fire in the Saltersgate Inn, near Whitby, England, which in the New Year celebrated 200 years of nonstop burning. Tradition says that disaster will strike the 400-year-old pub, which stands on the moors between the Devil's Elbow and the Hole of Horcum, if it ever goes out.

On occasions when the flames have burned low, pictures have fallen off the wall, appliances have switched themselves off and on and the beer has gone flat. Regulars will not venture into the pub if the fire is not roaring in the grate. "I've seen what can happen," said Mr. Milner. "A year ago a picture above the fireplace jumped off the wall. There's no way it should have happened. It was a big strong hook."

The tradition dates from 1796 when a customs officer was killed by smugglers and buried under the hearth. To avert the suspicions of the police, a fire was lit and kept burning. Should it ever go out, his spirit will be released to haunt the pub.

STRANGE DEATHS

☻ A man who stuffed two tampons up his nostrils to try and stop his snoring suffocated in his sleep on January 23. Laborer Mark Gleeson, 26, of Headley Down, England, had been told by doctors his snoring was incurable after a car crash eight years earlier left him with sinus problems. On the night he died, he was staying with his girlfriend Tracey Lambert. After drinking wine and taking a few sleeping tablets, he agreed to use the tampons and secured them with tape before going to sleep on her sofa.

☻ A 17-year-old Hong Kong girl was killed when a tethered balloon she was strapped to broke free and drifted 25 miles before bursting and throwing her to the ground. The body of the teenager, part of a tour group visiting a movie theme park in Panyu, China, was found five hours after the balloon took off.

☻ Fishing at night, Meli Kalakulu of Gao Island, Fiji, bled to death when a surface-skimming swordfish leapt at his lamp and stabbed him in the face.

☻ On March 17, Julianna Farkas, aged 80, leaned over a sauerkraut barrel to scoop out a portion, fell in and drowned. Farkas, an ethnic Hungarian from Oradea in Romania, was visiting relations in Ebes, a village 100 miles east of Budapest. Neighbors discovered the accident when they heard the woman's three-year-old great-grandson crying in the yard with no one attending him. It was assumed that Farkas was overcome by pungent cabbage fumes. The liquid in the barrel was a foot deep.

☻ A man of 75, walking his dachsund in Berlin on April 4, 1995, was attacked by a 43-year-old man who bit him on the neck, shouting "I am Dracula!" Passersby overpowered the attacker and handed him over to the police. He said he had been drinking. The victim went home and died an hour later from a heart attack.

UFOs

DUNKIN' UFOS

The South Korean air force monitored a doughnut-shaped object that hovered over a hilly park in Taegu, glowing with a luminous red light. Radio and TV were swamped with reports and a large crowd gathered to watch it move across the evening sky.

BRITISH AIRWAYS JET BUZZED BY UFO

A British Airways 707 encountered an unidentified wedge-shaped craft over the Pennines, according to a report by the Independent Joint Airmiss Working Group. At 6:48 p.m. on January 6, Flight 5061 from Milan was eight to nine nautical miles southeast of Manchester Airport with 60 people aboard. The encounter took place at 4,000 feet, just above the clouds. Although it was dark, visibility was at least six miles with a fairly strong northwest wind. Captain Roger Wills saw the speedy craft approach and pass silently down the starboard side of the plane in the opposite direction. Wills tracked it for about two seconds through the windscreen and side window, and thought it had a number of small white lights, rather like a Christmas tree. There was no apparent wake. The craft passed so close to them that his co-pilot, First Officer Mark Stuart, involuntarily ducked, although he remembers seeing a black stripe down its side.

Questioned, the two officers independently drew what they had seen, agreeing about the shape, but disagreeing about the lighting. Stuart felt that the object was illuminated by the jet's landing lights, which were at that stage switched on. The captain estimated the craft's size as somewhere between a light aircraft and a small jet, although he emphasized that this was pure speculation.

Here is an artist's depiction of the unidentified craft based on the pilots' descriptions.

Nothing was seen on the radar, but the flight officers are certain that the object was solid and not a balloon, model aircraft, or military stealth aircraft, which Stuart had seen before and would have recognized. "Enquiries into military activity," said the official report, "did not reveal any aircraft in that area at the time, and it was considered inconceivable that such activity would take place so close to a busy airport without some sort of prior notification." The report concluded that the incident "remains unresolved" and commented: "To speculate about extraterrestrial activity . . . is not within the Group's remit."

The greatest mystery is that the encounter was reported in the *Asian Age* under the headline: "Philippine nurse flies first class to become a mother."

CHINA SAUCER

Four aircraft flying over northeast China at about the same time reported seeing UFOs. The captain of a

Northern Airlines flight from Harbin to Beijing reported seeing a white oval UFO, which later turned green, traveling about 560 mph near his flight path on December 4. The captain of another civil aircraft reported the same thing, while two other airplanes spotted red or yellow UFOs.

ALIEN ROUTE

At the suggestion of Pat and Joe Travis, proprietors of the Little A'Le'Inn on Route 375 in the Nevada desert, Route 375 has been officially named the "Extraterrestrial Highway," a nod by the state's transportation board to the area's reputation for UFO sightings (Area 51/Groom Lake is nearby) and a ploy to attract tourists.

WHAT GOES THERE?

At an inquiry into June 2's fatal Chinook helicopter crash on the U.K.'s Mull of Kintyre, tapes of Prestwick Control Center radar screens were introduced to document a slow-moving object's presence around the time and the place of the crash. On January 22, Flight Lieutenant Hamish Miller said the object was moving north at 30–50 mph and could have been "a variety of things"—a slow-moving aircraft, a pocket of ionized air reflecting on radar, or a large flock of birds.

Could there be a sinister spin to this crash? Certainly, it was a major setback for the British security services in Northern Ireland: those killed included ten senior Royal Ulster Constabulary officers, nine army intelligence officers, six MI5 officials and the four-man RAF special forces crew. Sensitive information was inevitably lost for good that day.

MYSTERY EXPLOSIONS

Officials in Djibouti, on the Horn of Africa, have asked the United Nations to help them explain two explosions from UFOs seen over the Gulf of Aden on December 5 and 7, 1995. "A few days after the explosions, inhabitants came down with various ailments such as coughing, diarrhea, breathing difficulties and headaches," a government minister said. Children were the worst affected and several died. The low-flying objects were seen by many as they exploded, causing windows to shatter, but no debris from the explosions has been found. UN staff were unable to offer an explanation for the explosions.

ASIAN UFO

Crowds gathered in Malaysia's central Selangor State after alleged sightings of a UFO occupied by aliens with long ears and little red eyes. The UFO was said to be as big as a football field and several stories high, encircled by flashing red, orange and green lights.

HAUNTED HOUSING

The Kane family in Greenock, Scotland, were moved to new public housing in 1991 following a bout of violent poltergeist activity. Among the various manifestations Michelle Kane had to put up with were mysterious steam that would appear from nowhere, fill the room and vanish; clawing noises coming from within the bedroom; and the appearance of an unknown liquid which left furniture and other items soaking wet but evaporated within a matter of minutes. The liquid was seen by Mrs. Kane, two neighbors and Canon Ken Quine. Her six-year-old daughter Cheryl said that she had seen two shadowy figures fighting in the bedroom.

Eventually, Mrs. Kane arranged for a Catholic priest, a Church of Scotland minister and a group of Spiritualists to visit the house—separately, one hopes. In an effort to vanquish the spirit, the Spiritualists held a ceremony in the living room, during the course of which they recited the Lord's Prayer. According to Mrs. Kane: "The floor of the flat suddenly began to vibrate at speed. The couch some of us were sitting on began to shake." Sadly, none of this had any apparent effect on the haunting, and Mrs. Kane was eventually rehoused after enlisting the aid of the Reverend Peter Webster, a local minister. He explained: "I did something practical by getting in touch with the provost and getting Mrs. Kane rehoused. I'll say that something happened in that house which is beyond our human understanding."

Kathryn Meredith and her family were driven from their council house in Mid Glamorgan, Wales, by a frightening series of supernatural events. According to Mrs. Meredith, her house was built on the site of an old farm, and the nature of her haunting often reflected this. Pigs were seen in the garden, and a ghostly figure was seen sitting on one of the beds. Unplugged electrical appliances would turn on and off of their own accord. A cup exploded while Mrs. Meredith was holding it, cutting her face. More worryingly, an electric fire was thrown across the bedroom, and a french fry pan was put on to heat after the family had gone to bed.

Unluckily for Mrs. Meredith, the Rhondda housing authorities are more skeptical than those in Greenock, and refused to recognize them as homeless after they fled in panic. Rhondda Borough Council spokesman Mike Johnston explained: "Mrs. Meredith does have a property, even if she is no longer living there. If there was a problem with damp or tiles off or something, we could repair it, but we have no experience of this sort of thing."

OVER THE MOON ABOUT ALIEN ARCHAELOGY

Hoagland maintains that this is "The Shard," a mile-and-a-half-high spire of meteorite-eroded glass.

Richard Hoagland and his pressure group, Mars Mission, are dedicated to the belief that visual evidence of ancient artificial structures can be found on hundreds of archived NASA and Soviet lunar photographs, if you look hard enough.

On March 21, Hoagland called a press conference at the prestigious National Press Club in Washington, D.C. In what was billed as "the announcement of the millenium," he promised to reveal startling photographs (suppressed for 30 years by a frightened NASA) of astronauts walking amid ancient ruins on the Moon. The speakers comprised former NASA scientists, engineers and other researchers who, under the aegis of the Mars Mission—renamed, at the 11th hour, the Enterprise Mission—issued a challenge to the White House to open up NASA files on "alien artifacts" and other lunar enigmas.

Some of their intriguing claims that hint at alien technology of incomprehensible scale, are "The Castle," "a geometric, glittering glass object hanging more than nine miles

above the surface of the Moon," and a number of "glass-like, highly complex 'domes' " in various locations and states of ruin.

The world press was unmoved by the results of Hoagland's four-year research. The huge enlargements of tiny sections of official photographs made the all-important images indistinguishable from out-of-focus, pixilated blotches. Still, those who could see past the technical difficulties of a complex presentation were confronted with some fascinating material, like a 1960 report commissioned by NASA from the Brookings Institution. This report anticipated intercepting alien transmissions or artifacts of life forms on the Moon, Mars or Venus. It gravely concluded—drawing on examples of the many terrestrial cultures that have been shattered by contact with their technological superiors—that any contact with ETs could cause the "downfall of civilization on Earth."

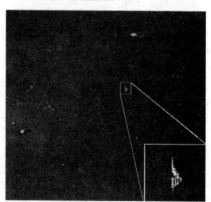

Hoagland produced this photo of "The Castle" suspended above the Moon's surface.

Richard Hoagland is in no doubt that the original purpose of President Kennedy's sudden, all-out Apollo Program was to get American astronauts to the lunar ruins first and to bring

FEEL A PRESENCE

❧ That redoubtable volume, *The Encyclopedia of Unusual Sex Practices,* lists among its many paraphilias the practice of spectrophilia—sexual arousal by intercourse with ghosts. It appears that some of those who have passed over to the spirit world are unwilling to be kept from the pleasures of the flesh by anything as simple as the lack of glands, hormones or indeed flesh.

❧ In 1994, Jill Cook of Blackwood, England, called in a priest, two psychics and even a Mormon missionary to try to help her get rid of a ghost which she claimed regularly sexually attacked her. The attacks began in early 1994, when she felt something climb into bed beside her and pull off the towel wrapped round her head. She heard a voice saying it was going to make love to her, and felt a "vile" sensation as it did so— "like tiny needles trying to pierce my skin." While she continued her quest to be rid of the haunting, she found that placing an ionizer in her room moved the ghost from one room to another.

❧ Elsewhere in England, Kent couple Sue and Ian Davies are plagued with a sex-hating phantom. The ghost apparently causes a racket every time they attempt intimacy, distracting them by groaning and banging on the walls. They believe the ghost is that of a former deep-sea diver whose friend used to live in their house, and believe that his campaign of disruption is aimed at preserving his peace and quiet—they thinks he hates the noise their children make, and wants to prevent them from having any more. They haven't yet managed to get rid of their unwelcome visitor, but have managed to find a temporary solution—a tent in the back garden. "It's chilly, but we have our love to keep us warm," said Ian. "The ghost is a real passion killer—and a better contraceptive than the Pill."

back any physical evidence they could find. Did the Brookings caution, and Cold War paranoia, cause Kennedy to cover up the success of the NASA lunar objectives, as Hoagland believes? "We are 30 years behind where we would have been," said Hoagland passionately. "It's time for the President to bite the bullet, to open NASA's files on all of this, and come clean."

Is our government suppressing the above as evidence of a "shattered crystalline city"?

CLOSE ENCOUNTERS & ALIEN ABDUCTIONS

ALIEN PRESENCE AT BOSNIA PEACE TALKS

According to the Internet, Richard Hoagland believes that Bosnian peace talk delegates were shown the bodies of aliens widely rumored to be preserved at Wright Patterson Air Base. Considering the ongoing crisis which brought the emissaries to the Dayton summit, why would such delegates be granted this privilege, let alone ask for it?

Bufo Calvin, whose E-mail newsletter supplied this nugget, proposes that such disclosure would show hostile parties from the former Yugoslavia how their minor tribal squabbles pale next to truly global concerns.

Hoagland is less coy: "We're being prepared for an interplanetary war."

IMPLANTS OUT OF THIS WORLD

The implant debate took off in two conflicting directions at the "Day of Abductions" conference in Sheffield, England, on April 20.

On the physical side, best-selling victim-author Whitley Strieber added specific details to the reports concerning two implants allegedly extracted from two separate residents of Houston, Texas, by Dr. Roger Leir. The investigators claimed that initial analysis has revealed tiny magnetic pieces of boron within the implants, surrounded by a tough organic membrane.

Strieber also commented on the opeations to remove the implants: "Everything in the surgeries was [recorded] on video. What's interesting is that local anaesthetic wasn't enough and the patients were also put under anaesthetic hypnosis."

Earlier in the proceedings, Pauline Delcour-Min, a hypnotic regressionist, had provided an explanation of why many reported implants fail to show up under medical examination. "Many implants are in the astral bodies," she said, pointing to a diagram showing different dimensions of existence. The implants exist, in effect, at a level above average human perception, she said. One wit, who wishes to remain anonymous, spoke up: "Nice one! It means we can't see the implants unless we believe in them."

IMPLANTS EXTRACTED

Dr. X, a surgeon in Ventura, California, who wished to remain anonymous, had been interested in ufology for five years when a Houston-based UFO researcher referred two unrelated people to him who believed they had been abducted by aliens. In both cases, objects of which the patients were unaware came to light in X rays for minor, unrelated injuries. "Neither bore any nearby scars or punctures," he said.

In August 1995, Dr. X was worried and said: "I'd probably be ostracized, I'd be criticized, maybe I'd even lose my license." He went on to explain: "People with credibility who put themselves forward in this field could wind up dead, in jail or out of business."

In decades of practice, said Dr. X, he'd never seen anything quite like the implants. They were encased in a thick, dark membrane. "These weren't cysts," he said, "They were so tough my scalpel wouldn't cut them."

When dried out and cut open, they revealed tiny, highly magnetic pieces of shiny black metal which glowed a brilliant green under ultraviolet light. The objects are said to be in Houston for electrical, chemical and microscopic analysis. The patients say they now feel liberated. Barry Karr, director of the Center for Scientific Investigation of Claims of the Paranormal, said: "Let's see the evidence."

ISN'T IT IRONIC?

❧ Kurt Svensson, 74, owner of a block of apartments in Grythyttan, Sweden, complained to the board of health about the large number of feral cats in the neighborhood. As a result, about 10 cats were shot dead by the police. The following day, a 41-year-old local (not named in the report) noticed that his cat, Knorre, was missing. Assuming that Svensson was to blame for his cat's death, the local threatened the senior's health. That evening, Svensson's block of apartments burned down; the local, found guilty of arson, was sentenced to eight years imprisonment.

The irony was that on the very night the man had taken out his revenge on Svensson, he found his beloved cat asleep in his living room. Moreover, due to his owner's imprisonment, the cat was to be put to sleep—until someone volunteered to care for the animal.

❧ Ralph Bregos waited two years for a heart transplant. When news arrived at his Kentucky home that a donor was available, Ralph, 40, got so excited that he had a massive heart attack and died.

❧ A man from England who had lived in Australia for 30 years returned to his home county in search of his long-lost brother, only to discover that the brother had emigrated—to Australia.

❧ Angie Jerston of Denver was touching up her lipstick as she drove to work when she was forced to brake sharply. The tube shot into her mouth and stuck in her windpipe. She died because she had locked the doors for safety and rescuers were unable to get in.

❧ Dorothy Dunn, 48, was fired from her job at Tameside General Hospital in England for taking three months sick leave—after being wrongly told she had angina by the same hospital.

❧ A married man and his lover stole away to a holiday cottage for a romantic evening. Hearing lively music nearby, they took some wine and joined the party. Inside, they found their own partners locked in embrace. The husbands intervened when the women tried to attack each other with garden hoes. Eventually, the men accompanied their own wives home amid cheers to their respective houses in Shoumen, Bulgaria.

WHERE'S MY SPACESHIP?

A man called Stephane, age 27, approached police in Montepellier, France, on January 24 for help in tracing his spaceship, which he claimed he had brought to Earth 350 years ago. The vessel was black, but he had misplaced its registration number. He needed to return to his planet to retrieve his guitar.

GALACTIC SNUB FOR BULGARIA

About 1,500 people gathered at an airfield near Shtraklevo in northern Bulgaria on September 11, awaiting the arrival of eight spaceships piloted by extraterrestrials from the planet Krissi.

The 11 a.m. landing had been foretold by three local mediums—Radka Trifonova, Zdravka Krumova and Ekaterina Nikiforova—who awaited along with the crowd, wearing identical dresses sewn especially for the great occasion.

The Earth was in danger of splitting in two, they said, but the beings from Krissi would avert the catastrophe. They would also help Bulgaria pay its crippling $12.9 billion foreign debt.

Half an hour after the scheduled arrival, the three mediums told the crowd that NATO warplanes flying in the region were scaring off the Krissiities.

After an hour had passed, they said that the aliens weren't coming because the Bulgarian president, Zhelyu Zhelev, had refused to come to the airfield to welcome them.

Police had to usher the women away from the angry crowd, although there was no violence.

BRAZIL NUTS OVER ALIENS

The hottest UFO story of the moment comes from Brazil, where it is rumored that a number of aliens have been recovered from a crashed UFO by military authorities. John Carpenter, a founder of the Institute for Contact with Non-Human Intelligence (ISCNI), enthused: "There are at least 35 first-hand witnesses to the presence of the strange beings. This includes audiotaped interviews with several military participants. There is the possibility of a UFO crash, but there is little doubt about the existence of five or six strange beings resembling a cross between the "little Greys" and the Chupacabras. Some were shot or died, others captured alive," he said.

This rendering reflects the "little Grey" and Chupacabras qualities of an alien allegedly captured in Brazil.

According to a press release dated June 9—issued by A.J. Gevaerd, president of the Brazilian Center for Flying Saucer Research—the story begins on the afternoon of January

20 near the city of Varginha when three young girls observed a strange creature in a field near their home. From a few yards away, they saw the creature squatting behind an old garage, apparently gasping in pain. When it made a slight movement, the girls fled. Although they saw no UFO, an elderly couple did claim later to have seen, earlier that morning, a grey, submarine-like object that silently skimmed the ground.

The girls were interviewed by Dr. Ubiraja Franco Rodrigues and Vitorio Pacaccini, two veteran ufologists who live in the vicinity. The two were quickly convinced by the description given by the unsophisticated witnesses that it was extraterrestrial. Its hairless body was not more than five feet tall and dark brown, as though it had oil on its skin. It had two large, red, pupil-less eyes, a small mouth and nose and a big, brown head with three rather rounded horns. It also smelled.

Rodrigues and Pacaccini located other Varginhans who had seen strange beings in the area and, at the same time, unusually intense military activity. A military informant told them that the fire department had been asked, early that morning, to capture a strange animal. On seeing it, they called the army base in the neighboring city of Tres Coracoes. The creature was finally netted, boxed and driven away on an army truck.

The commander, Lieutenant Colonel Olimpio Wanderley Santos, then declared it a "secret operation." However, the investigators were able to gather testimony from several military personnel. They spoke of the capture of a second creature—possibly the one seen by the girls later that night.

This second creature, apparently similar to the first, wound up at Humanitas Hospital. After two days, according to the story, the creature died and was removed at night by "S2" military intelligence officers. Anyone who saw the creature, it seems, was warned not to talk to the press and UFO researchers.

The investigators somehow learned that the aliens (dead or alive) were taken to a military facility in Sao Paulo. It is also alleged that one was autopsied at the University of Campinas. A six-month hunt for information has led to revisions of the number of witnesses and their stories, including the number of aliens. The latest version claims that five ETs were flushed out of a park on the north side of Varginha.

As luck would have it, a grand opportunity to go public came with the International Conference on UFOs, sponsored by Gevaerd's group over June 4–9. Key attendants were impressed by a special audience with Rodrigues and Pacaccini, who marshaled an array of eyewitnesses, including four soldiers who allegedly helped ferry the aliens to Sao Paulo. On June 5, the alleged Varginha retrieval was outlined for the press.

On Sunday, June 16, the TV show Programma de Domingo broadcast the story, identifying some of the military and civilian officials and interviewing witnesses. Furious at the leaks from his command, a General Lima confined his men; "What the ufologists say is ridiculous," he fumed. A spokesman for the East Military Area denies that any military personnel helped capture an alien: "We worry about national and international beings but only if they are terrestrials."

The case is developing the usual mythology. According to Luiza Helena, the mother of two of the girls, she was offered a large amount of cash by four unidentified men if her daughters would deny the story. It is believed that John Mack, a professor of psychiatry at Harvard Medical School who has specialized in treating abductees, came to Varginha to interview the girls. There are even rumors of U.S. involvement in the recovery and allegations that NORAD had tracked the craft. "By now, it is very likely that the body has already been flown from Brazil to the U.S.A.," said Pacaccini.

In recent years, Brazil has been a hotbed of UFO-related rumors. Of particular concern were the claims made by some ufologists of animal and even human vampiric mutilations—elsewhere attributed to the Chupacabras—based on evidence in police files. Meanwhile, according to Gevaerd, southern Minas Gerais, the home state of Varginha, is enduring one of the biggest UFO waves ever recorded, with many reports of close observations, landings and contact.

PARANORMAL EXPERIENCES

SHATTERING EXPERIENCE

At about 2 a.m. on May 7, Kerstin Lehtihet and her family were woken at their home in in Stockholm, Sweden, by a loud bang which also woke their neighbors. The glass table in their living room had exploded. Splinters of glass lay everywhere, including the bookshelves.

Camilla Walfridsson, assistant manager of Ikea, the department store where the table was bought two years ago, confirmed that glass furniture might explode, but she knew of only one previous incident: an exploding showcase. Usually the cause was tension created by a change in temperature resulting, for instance, from a hot coffee pot. Kerstin Lehtihet, however, said that nothing either hot or cold had been put on the table. The only things on it were a small tablecloth, a mug and an empty wooden bowl. The temperature was even, the windows were closed and there were no domestic pets that might have jumped on the table.

SHOCKING DRIP

Water started spouting from Guiseppe Galli's walls and electric sockets in Pesaro, Italy. A plumber could find nothing wrong; neither could the fire brigade, who suggested poltergeist trouble. Galli moved out and called a priest.

SKINNY

Bank robber Christopher Jeburk, 20, escaped through a window only seven inches wide in a jail in Appling, Georgia, and then scaled a 12-foot fence. Said a guard: "It is a puzzle how any human being could have fitted through such a tiny window." Perhaps Jeburk was like the flexible Eugene Tooms in *The X-Files*.

ALARMINGLY HOT

A fire alarm at the Moss Hospital in Norway caught fire on August 16, but the flames were quickly put out and there was little damage. The alarm was fixed to the ceiling in a corridor on the second floor and was smoke-reactive. The police and the fire department both visited the site, but left bewildered. "The charred fire alarm has been sent to a technician for examination and will, if necessary, be forwarded to the central forensic lab," said the police chief.

PECULIAR PRESS

A MILLION ETs GET NEW IDENTITY DEAL
Guardian, September 12, 1995

ORDER OF THE BOOT FOR ALIEN WORMS
Times, January 11, 1995

MOBILE PHONE THREAT TO UNIVERSE
Today, July 5, 1995

JUST A COINCIDENCE...?

🛸 A Plymouth, England audience for a lecture on "How to Cope with a Crisis" were told the speaker could not come—as his house was on fire.

🛸 Mark Merifield of Rushen, England, was 21 when he lost his right thumb on a meat cutter at the abattoir where he works. His father Martin, 48, also lost his right thumb at the age of 21 after an accident with a metal grinding machine.

🛸 Exchequer Court, an office building in London designed by Fitzroy Robinson, was structurally damaged one week before completion by the St. Mary Axe IRA bomb in 1992. The Fitzroy team was struck by how the bomb had damaged both the actual building and the architect's model (inside the building at the time of the explosion) in exactly the same place.

🛸 Jodie Bowler, 21, took the name of Mrs. Bowler-Hatt when she married baker Chris Hatt, 27, of Frinton, Essex.

🛸 Ann Bird, Pam Peacock and Tom Goose have been appointed regional organizers of the Royal Society for the Protection of Birds.

🛸 A production of *Singing in the Rain* was abandoned on June 6 after a fault in the sprinkler system poured hundreds of gallons of water into the playhouse.

🛸 Opera singer Richard Versalle, 63, died when he fell 10 feet from an onstage ladder while performing in *The Makropulos Case,* an opera about the secret of eternal life, at the Metropolitan Opera House in New York City. A heart attack is thought to be the cause for the fall; Mr. Versalle's final line was "Too bad you can only live so long."

MIC LEADS

A network of secret sea-floor microphones called SOSUS (sound surveillance system), installed by the United States during the Cold War to listen to the sound of Soviet submarines, is being opened for use by oceanographers. Besides the sounds of whales, fish, subterranean volcanoes and nuclear tests, there are several unidentified sounds that scientists call the "Echo," the "Carpenter" and the "Woof-Woof."

ELF INSURANCE

During work on a new road last September at Ljarskogar, north of Reykjavik, Iceland, bulldozers kept breaking down in front of one particular stone. The contractors accepted an offer from medium Regina, to see if it was a problem with elves. The message came through that elves no longer lived in the stone, but nearby. However, they wanted workers to remove it in a dignified manner, not just try to dig it up. Apparently, Regina's advice was followed and the mechanical problems ceased.

According to a recent survey, about ten percent of Icelanders believe in elves and other denizens of the spirit world; another ten percent deny them and the remaining eighty percent have no opinion or refuse to rule out their existence. "Our basic approach is not to deny the phenomenon," said Birgir Gudmundsson, an Iceland Road Authority engineer. "We tread very carefully. There are some people who can negotiate with the elves, and we make use of that."

One of the country's most famous elf-finders is a clairvoyant piano teacher and mother of three called Erla Stefansdottir. "I don't have to believe in these things," she said, "but I keep seeing them. I have always been seeing too much. When I walk down the street, I can't tell who is alive and who is dead of the people I meet. I must touch them to find out. I can meet myself on a highway 20 years ago. I can easily look back 1,000 years."

TANKS FOR CALLING

Every 90 minutes, day and night for six months, Donna Graybeal's phone in Billerica, Massachusetts, would ring. She picked up the receiver 2,688 times, to hear a rush of air, a click and a dial tone. Nobody was ever there. Police traced the calls to the home of Theodore and Elisabeth James of Potomac, Maryland; but they weren't calling Graybeal. The culprit was an old, unused heating oil tank that awoke unexpectedly in the basement and used an automatic dialing device to call an oil company to tell it

LOOK INTO MY EYES...

❡ In recent months, several thousand people in Indonesia have reported being robbed of money and valuables under hypnosis. "After a brief conversation with three men on the bus, I handed over all my jewelry," said Nesah, a 60-year-old West Java housewife. "I then got off with the men and took them home. Then I handed over my remaining jewelry and $400 in cash. I only fully regained consciousness four days later." Mamok, one of Indonesia's leading hypnotists, said that a person could be entranced in a few seconds and has warned against talking to strangers in public. According to a Jakarta police spokesman, this new form of robbery—typically committed in buses and shopping centers—was becoming increasingly common. No one has been arrested.

❡ In Colombia, hypno-thieves enhance the suggestibility of their victims by first drugging them. In Thailand, transvestite hypno-thieves are said to lace their nipples with tranquilizers.

❡ On April 16, 1992, a man hypnotized a cashier at the Banca Nazionale del Lavoro in Reggio, Calabria, Italy, into giving him $4,000. The bank robber escaped.

its fuel was low. Steuart Petroleum in Washington installed the re-dialer device in a short-lived test. The tank was dialing an 800 number that Steuart dropped several years ago.

Nobody knows what brought the oil tank to life. Harold Herman, a Bell Atlantic Corporation cable maintenance supervisor who traced the calls, said that it might have been either a power surge or a lightning strike.

CORNISH HUM

A mysterious humming sound has been plaguing Cornwall, England, residents as far apart as Praa Sands and Penzance. Ernie Williams of Praa Sands had noticed the persistent "thrumming" background noise for some months. His wife Pat said they had driven around to see if they could discover its cause, but the noise seemed worse inside the house with all the doors and windows shut. "At first I thought I had tinnitus," she said, "but friends who have come to the house can hear it clearly. Even my husband, who is quite deaf, can hear it plainly."

Elanor Taylor of Penzance said that she had heard a hum inside her house since August and it disturbed her sleep. She could not hear it outdoors. She suspected the new sewage system installed by South West Water, but an engineer there remarked that if the noise was as bad as Mrs. Taylor suspected, more people would have complained.

DAZED AND CONFUSED

Two teenage girls who were hypnotized at a seaside show in Lankenberge, Belgium, a year ago haven't been seen since. The hypnotist used voodoo dolls and persuaded the embarrassed girls that they were naked in front of 800 people. After the show, An Marchal, 17, and her pal Eefje Lambrecks, 19, were filmed by a security camera wandering around like zombies. Later they caught a train to Ostend. The police have no clues.

SOURCES

THE HUMAN WORLD

Strange Behavior 4

Walk the Tube: *[New Zealand Press Association]*, May 11, 1996.

Snuff Stiff: *Daily Star*, April 27, 1995.

Hello Deer: *[Associated Press]*, December 7, 1995.

Talking Penis Axed: *Sussex Evening Argus*, September 20, 1995.

Monuments of Invention: *Aberdeen Press & Journal*, August 11, 1995.

All You Can Eat: *Sunday Mail*, September 17; October 8, 1995.

Creepy Clowns: *Daily Telegraph*, November 3, 1995; *Independent on Sunday*, November 5, 1995; *Washington Times*, June 7–11, 1994; *Washington Post*, June 9–13, 1994; *Alexandria* (Virginia) *Journal*, June 10, 1994; *Prince George's Journal* (Maryland), June 13, 1994; *Minneapolis Star Tribune*, May 27, 1992; *Daily Telegraph, Guardian, Independent*, October 6, 1995.

Sanity Clause: *[AP]*, June 22, 1995.

Veiled Threat: *[Agence France Press]*, January 4, 1996.

I'm Gonna Get You Suckler: *[AP]*, April 23, 1996.

Rocky Remedy: *Wolverhampton Express & Star*, October 16, 1995.

Dental Decor: *Sunday Mail*, July 23, 1995.

In the Name of God: *[AP]*, February 15, 1996.

Veggie Specials: *Evening Standard*, April 19, 1996; *Sunday Express*, September 17,1995; *[AP]*, February 9, 1996.

Color Blind: *Daily Telegraph*, September 28, 1995.

Tools: *[AP]*, December 28, 1995; *Daily Record*, July 10, 1995.

Wanted—Goldilocks: *Daily Record*, September 15, 1995.

Tumbled: *The Tennessean*, January 19, 1996.

Bit of a Ding Dong: *[AFP]*, March 11, 1996.

Natural State: *Black Country Evening Mail*, May 1, 1996.

Appetite Sharpener: *[AFP]*, June 7, 1996.

Got a Light?: *[AP]*, *[Reuters]*, February 2, 1996.

Two Left Feet: *North County Register* (Hamilton, Ontario), June 1996.

Dough for Brains: *Denver Post*, April 6, 1996; e-mail from bemo@eclipse.co.uk (Ben Morrish), June 4, 1996.

Mad Manaclers: *Western Morning News*, June 10, 1996.

Off the Rails: *New York Daily News*, May 6, 1996.

Math Is Murder: *[AFP]*, June 5, 1996.

Cross Purposes: *Daily Telegraph*, May 17, 1996; *Sunday Telegraph*, November 12, 1995; *The Times* (of Malta), December 11, 1995; *Norwich Evening News*, April 8, 1996.

You're Grounded!: *Evening Standard*, March 25, 1996; *Daily Mail*, March 26, 1996; *Daily Mirror*, March 26, 1996; *Sunday Times*, April 28, 1996; *Halifax Evening Courier*, April 29, 1996.

Just Launder: *[R]*, June 2, 1996.

Cement Sacrifice: *Independent*, July 4, 1996.

Loafer: *Times* (London), June 13, 1996.

Wait in Vain: *Daily Record*, March 18, 1996.

Great Escapes: *Sunday Mail* (Scotland), July 23, 1995; *Daily Mail*, August 19, 1996.

Dog Told Me To: *[AP]*, August 3, 1996.

Artful Roger: *Daily Telegraph*, June 19, 1996.

Eye Caramba!: *Western Morning News*, April 6, 1996; *Hong Kong Eastern Express*, May 7, 1996.

Timely Resurrection: *Daily Telegraph*, January 6, 8, 9, and 11, 1996; *Sunday Telegraph*, January 7, 1996; *[AFP]*, December 15, 1995; *South China Morning Post*, December 19, 1995; *Daily Mirror*, March 4, 1996; *Johannesburg Star*, March 24, 1995; *Wolverhampton Express & Star*, October 16, 1995; *Daily Telegraph*, October 16,

1995; *Brisbane Courier Mail,* October 18, 1995.

Kermitted: *Eastern Evening News,* March 22, 1996.

Cults and Conspiracies 14

The Most Evil Politician: *Richmond & Twickenham Times,* January 19, 1996.

Echoes of the Past Haunt Train Wreck: *[UPI],* October 11, 1995; *Guardian,* October 13, 1995; *Dallas Morning News,* October 21, 1995.

Kneecaps Nabbed: *[R],* April 12, 1994; August 7, 1995.

Kids Today . . . : *USA Today,* December 5, 1995.

Satancalifragilistic: *Sunday Express,* September 17, 1995.

Kennedy Assassin Fesses Up: *Guardian,* June 11, 1996.

Green Party, Black Magic: *News of the World,* April 28, 1996; *Times,* June 13, 1996; *Sunday Mirror,* July 7, 1996.

Legal Lunacy: *Evening Standard,* May 14, 1996; *Wolverhampton Express & Star,* August 23, 1995; December 7, 1995; *Daily Record,* January 16, 1996; *Daily Record,* March 21, 1996.

Police Postpone Doomsday: *[R],* September 29, 1995.

Deaths and Suicides 17

When the Bough Breaks: *Sunday Express,* December 31, 1995.

Hare and Gone: *Hong Kong Standard,* January 8, 1996.

Mystery Comes Out in the Wash: *Saga* magazine, via *Daily Telegraph,* July 7, 1995.

Poor Execution: *[AP],* September 15, 1994.

Money Where Your Mouth Is: *Albuquerque Journal,* April 29, 1995; *Sydney Herald-Sun,* March 2, 1996.

Landing Fear: *New York Post,* May 24, 1996; *Houston Chronicle,* May 24, 1996.

Maybe It's Your Personality, Pal: *Times,* February 14, 1995.

Boom Town: *[AFP],* March 10, 1996.

What Were Those Ten Thingies Again?: *[AP],* July 20, 1996.

Out of Season: *Ivoir' Soir* [Ivory Coast], December 29, 1994.

Cappers: *Western Morning News,* July 24, 1996; *Daily Telegraph,* July 6, 1996.

Flossed Cause: *South China Morning Post,* April 27, 1996.

Weather or Not, He's Responsible: *Hong Kong Eastern Express,* January 20, 1996.

Dead Dad Starts Trend: *Eastern Evening News,* July 11, 1996.

Plumming the Deaths: *Nottingham Evening Post,* August 8, 1996.

Computer Error: *Daily Record,* April 18, 1996; *People,* April 28, 1996.

Tape Head: *[AP],* June 12, 1996.

The Reaper Rings Twice: *Times, Daily Express,* February 23, 1996; *[AP],* January 16, 1996; *Daily Telegraph,* February 26, 1996; *[AP],* February 20, 1996; *La Repubblica,* November 9, 1995; *Daily Telegraph,* November 10, 1995.

Fish Gag: *Houston Chronicle,* July 8, 1996.

Stardust: *Sunday Express,* June 2, 1996; *Daily Record,* June 11, 1996.

Terror in Peru: *[R],* August 5, 1996; *International Herald Tribune,* August 22, 1996.

Method Acting: *[AP],* May 15, 1996.

Pest Control: *Edinburgh Evening News,* March 19, 1996.

Zero Sum Game: *Sunday Express,* December 10, 1995.

Meat Me in St. Petersburg: *[R],* September 2, 1995; *Sunday Times,* September 10, 1995; *[AP],* July 8, 25, 1995; *[R],* May 9, 1996; *[AFP],* February 8, 1996; *[R],* February 9, 1996; *Hong Kong Eastern Express,* March 4, 1996; *[AP],* October 3, 1995; *[AP],* June 5, 9, 1995; *Coventry Evening Telegraph,* November 27, 1995.

Genius and Discovery 23

You Must Remember This: *Coventry Evening Telegraph, Daily Mail, Daily Telegraph,* July 18, 1996.

Head Rush: *New York Times*, July 2, 1996; *Asian Age* (New Delhi), July 9, 1996.

Where Does It Hurt?: *Glasgow Herald*, January 13, 1996.

Family with "Gills": *Cork Examiner*, July 27, 1996.

Nose Picking Is Sexy: *[Knight-Ridder]*, November, 1991; *Journal of Clinical Psychiatry*, February 1995.

Water Power Baffles Scientists: *[AFP]*, November 3, 1995.

Head Lines: *Glasgow Herald*, January 13, 1996.

Birthday Surprise: *Evening Standard*, April 3, 1996; *West Briton*, April 25, 1996; *Halifax Evening Courier*, November 15, 1995; *Western Daily Press*, *Daily Mirror*, March 4, 1996; *Sheffield Star*, April 25, 1996.

Snail Mail: *Daily Telegraph*, July 20 and July 27, 1994; *Daily Mail*, July 27, 1994; Victoria (British Columbia) *Times-Colonist*, January 27, 1996; *Daily Mirror*, November 29, 1991; *The Nation* (Thailand), November 30, 1991; *Edinburgh Evening News*, December 14, 1991; *New Zealand Dominion Sun-Times*, December 15, 1991; *Leicester Mercury*, March 8, 1994; *[R]*, April 6, 1996; *Hackensack* (N.J.) *Record*, March 9, 1995; *Independent on Sunday*, January 30, 1994.

Hoaxes and Panics 27

Volcano Panic: *La Paix* (Ivory Coast), November 8, 1995.

Shades of Orson Welles: *The Dominion* (Wellington, N. Z.), May 18, 1996.

Take Me to Your Bedroom: *Los Angeles Times*, September 16, 1995.

Husband Hacking Sham: *Guardian*, June 20, 1996.

Unwelcome Wagon: *[AP]*, September 1994; *Weekly News*, October 8, 1994.

Bilking Birdbrains: *Daily Telegraph*, July 24, 1995.

When Gonads Are Goners: *[AP]*, August 22, 1996.

Dud: *Morning Star, Sussex Evening Argus*, October 27, 1995.

Flights of Fancy: *[AFP]*, August 9, 1995.

Bag o' Wife: *Daily Mirror*, March 1, 1996; *Sunday Telegraph*, March 10, 1996.

So Stupid It's Criminal: *[R]*, *Daily Telegraph*, August 5, 1996; *Daily Record*, June 11, 1996; *Western Daily Press*, January 27, 1996; *Daily Telegraph*, June 1, 1996; *Times*, June 1, 1996; *Guardian*, June 1, 1996; *Times*, December 16, 1996.

Ineptitude and Stupidity 30

Cleaned Out: *[AP]*, August 26, 1994.

Dummies: *[AFP]*,[AP], April 1, 1996.

Radio Gaga: *New Scientist*, January 20, 1996.

Naked As a Jailbird: *[UPI]*, June 7, 1996.

Byewatch: *Independent on Sunday*, September 10, 1995.

Die Hards: *[AP]*, April 23, 1996; *China Post*, April 23, 1996; *San Jose Mercury News*, August 6, 1994; *Guardian*, July 11, 1996; *Daily Telegraph*, July 25, 1995; *Daily Mirror*, July 26, 1995; *[AP]*, March 20, 1996; *[R]*, May 2, 1996.

Strongarmed: *Guardian*, October 17, 1995.

Dead Wrong: *Aberdeen Press and Journal*, December 26, 1992; *Independent*, January 8, 1993.

Funeral Follies: *Electronic Telegraph*, March 27, 1996; *Daily Mirror*, January 5, 1996.

Antiquities 33

Buddha's Birthplace Revelation: *Daily Telegraph*, February 5, 1996; *San Francisco Chronicle*, February 6, 1996; *South China Morning Post*, February 6, 1996; *Times*, February 6, 1996.

First Call: *Nature*, June 6, 1996; *Times*, June 6, 1996; *International Herald Tribune*, June 7, 1996.

Steel Works: *Nature*, January 1996; *Guardian*, January 11, 1996; *New York Times*, February 6, 1996.

Charlesfort Found: *Daily Telegraph*, June 7, 1996; *Guardian*, June 7, 1996.

The Rabbit and the Crab: *Science et Vie*, May 1991.

Shroud in Controversy: *[AP]*, May 22, 1996; *USA Today*, May 22, 1996; *Houston Chronicle*, May 26, 1996.

Iconoclast Seeks Job: *International Herald Tribune*, June 3, 1996; *Independent*, June 6, 1996.

Dirty Laundry: *Observer*, April 21, 1996; *Guardian*, April 24, 1996; *Independent*, April 30, 1996.

Shoe-In: *Guardian, Daily Telegraph*, July 8, 1995.

Hurrian Home: *[AP]*, November 21, 1995; *Providence Journal*, December 24, 1995; *Daily Mail*, March 25, 1996.

Coining It: *[AFP]*, August 3, 1996.

Political Asylum: *[AP]*, January 28, 1996; *German News* (English Edition), June 5, 1996; *Edmonton Sun*, October 11, 1995; *Guardian*, February 1, 1996; *Irish Times* online, April 23, 1996; *Daily Telegraph*, January 19, 1996.

....

THE ANIMAL WORLD
....

Out-of-Place Animals 40

Shockoli: *Evening Standard*, June 19, 1996; *Times*, June 20, 1996.

Raining Cats and Cats: *Weekend Telegraph*, September 24, 1994.

Rectal Rodent: *BMA Journal*, May 1996.

Sofa, So Good: *Victoria Times-Colonist*, February 11, 1996.

Trained Pigeons: *Midweek*, June 5, 1995; *New Scientist*, September 2, 16, 30, 1995; *Daily Telegraph*, September 29, 1995; *Daily Mail*, September 30, 1995.

Survivors: *Times*, July 13, 1996; *Ivoir' Soir*, December 29, 1994.

Cassock Commotion: *Electronic Telegraph, Home News*, May 3, 1996.

Dogged Journeys: *[AFP]*, January 7, 1996; *Hong Kong Standard*, March 10, 1996; *[AFP]*, January 7, 1996; *Hong Kong Standard*, March 10,

1996; *[R]*, April 27, 1996; *Western Morning News*, March 2, 1996.

Turtle Travels: *Daily Mail, Guardian*, February 26, 1996.

Smuggle Up: *[AFP]*, September 28, 1995; *Daily Record*, May 14, 1996.

I Think I've Got a Bite: *Times*, August 16, 1996.

Otter Splatter: *Mail on Sunday*, August 27, 1995.

P.O.'d: *European*, January 27, 1995.

Boarish Behavior: *Times*, March 21, 1996.

Attacks by Animals 44

Lover Bulls: *Expressen* (Sweden), May 31, 1996; *Sydsvenska Dagbladet*, June 7, 1996.

Pet Food: *[AP]*, March 7, 1996; *Houston Chronicle*, March 7, 1996; *Daily Mirror*, March 7, 1996.

Goosed: *[R]*, December 16, 1995.

Really Mad Cow Disease: *Oxford Star*, May 23, 1996.

Snake Bitten: *[AP]*, May 11, 1996.

Knock Your Spots Off: *Yorkshire Post*, July 17, 1995.

Held Hostage by Rook Rage: unavailable.

Animal Anomalies: *[R]*, May 9, 1996; *Daily Telegraph, Daily Mail*, March 23, 1996; *Daily Mail*, November 14; *Politiken* (Denmark), November 22, 1995.

Cats Underfoot: *Daily Telegraph*, May 30, 1996; *Western Morning News*, May 30, 1996; *Aberdeen Evening Express*, April 27, 1996.

Fish Story: *[AP]*, June 17, 1996.

Trapper John: *News of the World*, May 26, 1996.

Fatal Error: *Newsweek*, October 2, 1995.

Feeding Time: *Victoria Times-Colonist*, June 19, 1996.

Python Tries to Swallow Man: *New Straits Times* (Malaysia), September 6-8, 1995; *Straits Times* (Singapore), September 7, 9, 1995.

Batty: *[R]*, April 3, 1996.

Go Wild!: *Toronto Star*, March 13, 1996; *Bangkok Post*, June 8, 1993.

Poodle Snatchers Take Flight: *Lewiston* (Maine) *Sun-Journal,* January 17; *Daily Star,* July 25, 1995.

Terrors of the Deep: *Aberdeen Press and Journal, Daily Telegraph,* September 2; *Borders on Sunday* (Carlisle), *News of the World,* September 3, 1995.

Hard Bitten: *Daily Mail,* June 22, 1996.

Attacks on Animals 49

Loved to Death: *Daily Telegraph,* October 17, 1995.

Murder Most Fowl: *Denver Post,* June 29, 1996; *Philadelphia Inquirer,* July 1, 1996; *Independent,* July 6, 1996.

Snake Harmer: *[AP],* January 24, 1996.

Dial-a-Fish Nets Catch in Borneo: *[AP],* April 25, 1996.

Wild at Heart: Evening *Times,* June 6, 1996.

Moo-tilation: *Newsletter* (Belfast), October 20, 1995.

Animal vs. Animal: *Mail on Sunday,* March 17, 1996; *[AFP],* December 16, 1995; *Rocky Mountain News,* June 17, 1996.

Man Bites Dog: *[AP],* June 13, 1996.

"Demon" Crocodiles Burn to Death: *[R],* *Ethiopian Herald,* September 24, 1995.

Monkey Business: *[AP],* December 15, 1995.

Animal Crackers: *Daily Mirror,* August 26, 1995; *Victoria Times*-Columnist, December 24, 1991, January 12, 1992, April 15, 1994, August 6, 1992, February 13, 1993; *Daily Mail, Daily Mirror, Wolverhampton Express & Star,* March 4, 1995.

Swarmings 53

Insectovision: *News of the World,* January 14, 1996.

Snails on the Rails: *[AP],* May 16, 1996.

Frog March: *Rocky Mountain News,* July 25, 1995.

What a Buzz: *Daily Mail,* July 26, 1996.

Go Wild!: *Guardian,* June 24, 1996; *Daily Telegraph, Daily Post,* November 9, 1993.

Heroic Animal: *[R],* July 31, 1995; *Las Provincias* (Spain), September 14, 1995; *Daily Telegraph,* August 27, 1996; *Guardian,* December 28, 1994; *[R],* July 25, 1996; *Daily Telegraph,* July 25, 1996.

New Species Found 55

It's a New Mammal: *New York Times,* February 20, 1996; *International Herald Tribune,* February 22, 1996.

Life, But Certainly Not As We Know It: *Guardian, Daily Telegraph, Austin American Statesman,* December 14, 1995; *Daily Mail,* December 15, 1995; *New Scientist,* December 16, 1995.

Keeping an Eye on the Signs of the Thai: *[AFP],* July 25, 1996.

Serpentine Tales: *Sydsvenskan,* August 10, 11, 1994; *Sydsvenska Dagbladet,* March 25, 1995; *[UPI],* February 22, 1995; *Philadelphia Inquirer,* September 17, 1996; *[AP],* June 22, 1994.

Two-toise: Unavailable.

Mass Deaths 57

All Washed Up: *Daily Yomiuri,* January 7, 1996; Japan *Times,* January 8, 1996.

Manimals 58

Spring-Heeled Jack in India: *[UPI],* June 26, 1996.

Dwarf Batman Terrorizes Zanzibar: *Guardian,* October 2, 1995.

Quickfoot Sighted in Scotland Forest: The *People,* November 12, 1995.

Gotta Have Ewe: *Times,* March 25, 1996; *New Zealand Herald, Eastern Express,* February 24, 1996.

Hollers Prompt Hairy Manhunt: *[AP],* November 6, 1995; *Columbus Dispatch,* November 3, 6, 1995; *National Enquirer,* January 16, 1996; *Guardian,* January 23, 1996; *Charlotte Observer,* January 28, 1996; *Los Angeles Times,* February 4, 1996; *Denver Post,* March 9, 1996.

Yeti Again: *Sunday Telegraph,* July 21, 1996.

Bloodsucker Spooks Puerto Rico: *Liverpool Echo,* November 20; *New York Daily News,* November 22, 1995.

Heroic Animals: *Carmarthen Journal,* August 28, 1996; *Daily Mail, Daily Telegraph,* August 30, 1996; *Daily Mail, Daily Telegraph,* April 4, 1996; *[AP],* August 17, 1996; *Sunday Times,* August 18, 1996; *Victoria Times-Colonist,* August 22, 1996.

Call of the Mild: *Today,* November 15, 1993; *[AP],* March 13, 1996; *Daily Mail, Daily Mirror,* April 22, 1993; *[R],* July 19, 1993; *New York Post,* January 15, 1992; *[AP],* May 14, 1996.

Wild Ideas: *[AFP],* May 27, 1996.

Water Monsters 64

Whole Loch of Sightings Going On: *Aberdeen Evening Express, Daily Mirror,* March 9, 1996; *Glasgow Herald,* April 17, 1996; *[R], Dundee Evening Telegraph,* June 15, 1996.

Monster Machinations: *Expressen,* July 21, 1996.

Impersonations: *China Daily,* June 26, 1995; *Daily Telegraph,* May 16, 22, 1996; *Daily Mail,* May 16, 1996.

Dinner, Not Diner: *[PA News],* August 2, 1996.

The Beast of Benbencula: *Newcastle Journal,* August 21, 1996; *Daily Telegraph, Birmingham Mail,* August 22, 1996.

Sea Monsters: *Eastern Daily Press,* June 3, 1996.

From Hull or Hell?: *Daily Mail,* October 6, 1995.

Horned and Hairy Turkish Terror: *[AP],* November 2, 1995.

Dogs and Cats Living Together: *[AP],* July 18, 1996; *[AP],* June 26, 1996; *Wolverhampton Express & Star,* April 9, 1996; *Daily Mail,* May 4, 1996; *Birmingham Evening Mail,* May 4, 1996.

THE NATURAL WORLD

Disasters, Natural & Man-Made 70

Fire in the Mountains: *Liberation,* January 26, February 7, 1996; *Guardian,* January 27, February 2, 6, 1996; *Times,* January 30, February 6, 1996; *Irish Times,* January 31, 1996; *Daily Express,* February 2, 1996; *[AP],* February 5, 7, 1996.

Tree Causes Massive Chaos: *[AP],* July 3, 22, 1996; *New York Times,* July 3, 1996; *Guardian,* July 4, 1996.

Disastair: *Times,* August 2, 1996.

Biological and Medical 72

Galling: *Daily Mirror,* March 15, 1996.

Sober Water: *[AP],* May 16, 1996.

Bust Bounce: *Independent on Sunday,* April 28, 1996.

Pardon?: *Sunday Mail,* June 2, 1996.

Roach Motel: *[R],* February 28, 1996; *[AP],* February 28, 1996.

Well Endowed: *Daily Record,* May 24, 1996; *Sunday Express,* May 26, 1996.

Yule Sprig Pulled from Teen's Lung: *[AP],* December 15, 1995.

The Living Dead of San Bernardo: *[R],* December 9, 1994; *[AP],* May 24, July 20, 1995.

Tiny Twin: *Bangkok Post,* October 19, 1992; *Asian Age,* December 22, 1994; *South China Morning Post,* January 7, 1995; *[AP],* June 1995; *[United Press International],* January 1993.

Curious Corpse: *[R],* April 18, 1996.

Wild Medicine: *Guardian,* September 12, 1995.

Late Deliveries: *The Lancet,* March 8, 1995; *[R],* March 18, 1995; *Daily Sport,* October 21, 1993; *Riyadh Daily,* April 6, 1995.

Eagle Eyes: *Scottish Sunday Mail,* January 28, 1996.

In Black and White: *Times,* July 10, 1996; *Glasgow Herald,* July 10, 1996; *Wolverhampton Express & Star,* July 10, 1996.

Livin' Large: *New York Post*, May 18, 21, 1996; *Daily Telegraph*, May 18, 1996; *New York Times*, May 19, 1996; *Victoria Times-Colonist*, May 19, 1996.

Right Under Our Noses: *International Herald Tribune*, February 15, 1996; *New Scientist*, February 24, 1996; BMJ, March 2, 1996.

Big Boy: *[AP]*, *New York Post*, August 13, 1996; *New York Daily News*, August 13, 14, 1996.

I'm Feeling Much Better, Doctor: *New Scientist*, September 2, 1995; *Toronto Globe and Mail*, September 9, 1995.

Pick Your Brains: *[AP]*, June 8, 1995.

Cyster: *[AP]*, February 22, 1996.

When Nair Won't Do: *[AP]*, August 27, 1996.

Suture Self: *[AFP]*, November 19, 1995.

More Seeds of Time: *[AP]*, August 14, 1995.

High Drama: *Guardian*, May 23, 1995; *Times*, May 24, 1995; *[AP]*, December 8, 1995.

Epidemics and Illness 80

Getting the Point: *Sunday Mirror*, February 21, 1993; *Western Mail*, November 16, 1994.

Allergic to Computers: *Sussex Evening Argus*, October 28, 1995.

Plague by Rumor: *Economist*, November 19, 1994; *Indian Express* (New Delhi), December 22, 1995.

Getting the Point: *[Tass]*, March 4, 1993; *Middlesbrough Evening News*, July 20, 1993; *Daily Telegraph*, July 21, 1993; *Daily Star*, *Sun*, January 13, 1994.

Class Trips: *[R]*, June 27, 1996; *Western Morning News*, June 27, 1996.

Top of the Pox: *Guardian*, August 31, 1993, October 31, 1994, February 2, 1995; *Daily Telegraph*, January 26, 1996.

Great Balls of Fire: Japan *Times*, *Evening Standard*, January 8, 1996; *Guardian*, January 11, 1996; *Dundee Courier*, February 15, 1996; *Boston Herald*, February 7, 1996; *Attleboro Sun-Chronicle*, February 7, 9, 1996.

Circles Crop Up All Over Europe: *Prague Post*, August 9–15; *Algemeen Dagblad*, August 11, 1995.

The Awful Tooth: *New York Daily News*, *Daily Telegraph*, October 28, 1995.

Another Reason to Stop Eating Chimp: *[R]*, February 19, 1996.

More Than Double Your Pleasure: *New York Times*, July 10, 1996; *International Herald Tribune*, July 11, 1996.

Growin' Up Too Fast: *[R]*, May 25, 1996.

Dragon Dung Disaster: *[AP]*, March 1, 1996.

Falls from the Sky 85

Something Fishy: unavailable.

Snow Drifts: *Morning Star*, July 23, 1996; *Victoria Times-Colonist*, July 24, 1996.

Water Bomb: *Morning Star*, July 23, 1996; *Victoria Times-Colonist*, July 24, 1996.

Plane Pellet: *Yorkshire Evening Post*, March 8, 1995.

Fall Guy: *Daily Telegraph*, *Times*, April 17, 1996; *Guardian*, *West Daily Press*, *Daily Telegraph*, May 31, 1995; *San Jose Mercury News*, May 13, 1995; *Daily Telegraph*, *Wolverhampton Express & Star*, August 30, 1994; *Daily Express*, March 29, 1996; *Edinburgh Evening News*, March 30, 1996.

Heaven Sent: *Sunday Telegraph*, February 18, 1996.

What Goes Up: *Independent*, February 5, 1996; *Times*, March 8, 1996; *Sunday Times*, March 10, 1996; *Daily Telegraph*, March 13, 1996.

A Gift from Above: *Weekend Telegraph*, November 19, 1994.

Frogstorm: *Sunday Mail*, October 22, 1995.

Strange Deaths: *[AP]*, January 4, 1996; *[AFP]*, February 28, 1996; *[AP]*, February 7, 1996.

Tears of the Gods: *Sheffield Star*, March

18, 1996.
Surround Sound: *Wolverhampton Express & Star,* May 21, 1996.

Meteorological Superlatives 89
On the Rocks: unavailable.
When It Rains . . . :unavailable.
Fertility Seats: *Wall Street Journal,* May 4, 1994; *Independent on Sunday,* May 15, 1994; *Yediot Aharonot,* May 31, 1994; *Daily Post,* May 16, 1995; *Daily Telegraph,* January 21, 1996; *WWW World News Today,* January 22, 1996.
Still Hotter: unavailable.
The Big Chill: unavailable.

Cosmological Superlatives 91
Rings Around the Sun: *Sussex Argus,* May 2, 1996.
One-Man–Band Pulsar: *Times,* February 26, 1996; *Independent,* November 1, 1996; *New Scientist,* March 2, 1996.
Comet Hyakutake X Rays Baffle Scientists: *Independent,* February 8, 1996; *Daily Telegraph,* February 9, March 21, 26, 1996; *New York Times,* March 16, 27; *Sunday Telegraph,* March 31; *Austin American Statesman,* April 5, 1996.
Galileo at Ganymede: unavailable.
Aries to Blame for Rams on the Road: *Daily Telegraph, Daily Express,* March 23, 1995.

Geophysical Activity 93
Mountain Mourning: unavailable.
Running Late: unavailable.
Not-So-Solid Ground: unavailable.
Mystery Holes in Frozen Lake: *Posten* (Gothenburg, Sweden), December 30, 1995.
It's a Yam's World: *The Times* (of Malta), February 1, 1996; *Daily Graphic* (Ghana), April 26, 1996.
Rangoon Ruby: *[AP],* May 16, 1996.
Much Too Mush: *[AFP],* July 29, 1996.
Dune Croon: *Observer,* December 3, 1995.

Psychical Phenomena 98
Cyberspoons: unavailable.
Twined Twins: *[AP],* May 27, 1996; *Daily Mail,* May 28, 1996; *Daily Telegraph* (New South Wales), May 28, 29, 1996; *Canberra Times* (ACT), May 28, 30, 1996.
Strange Deaths: *Daily Mail,* November 10, 1995; *Daily Mail,* November 27, 1995; *[R],* November 11, 1995; *Los Angeles Times,* August 17, 1994; *[AP],* November 25, 1995.
Mind over Matter: *Daily Telegraph,* October 28, 1991, January 8, 1992, September 21, 1994, April 27, May 3, 1995; *New Scientist,* March 20, 1992, August 27, September 3, 1994; *New Statesman and Society,* August 19, 1994, September 3, 1994, April 7, 1995; *Guardian,* September 1, 1994, March 30, April 20, October 2, 5, 1995; *Sunday Express,* October 1, 1995; *Sunday Times,* October 1, 1995; *Independent,* October 2, 1995.
Clairvoyant Foresaw Own Death: *New York Times,* April 5, 1995; *[R],* August 8, 1995; *[AP],[AFP],* August 11, 1995; *Times,* August 14, 1996.

Prophecies 102
Antichristmas: *New York Times,* June 6, 1996; *Houston Chronicles,* June 8, 1996.
Killer Mammaries Doomed to Drop: *Time,* March 18, 1996.
Scales of Fate: *Economist,* September 2, 1995.
Qabbalah Curse Clue to Rabin Murder: *New York Post,* November 7, 1995; *Jerusalem Report,* November 16, 1995.
Diamond Discoveries: *Daily Record, Daily Mirror,* April 26, 1996; *Weekly News,* July 27, 1996; *Daily Record,* February 1, 1994; *Sunday Mail*

(Scotland), July 11, 1993.

Doth the Vatican Protest Too Much?: *Ivoir' Soir,* October 27, 1995.

Apparitions 104

Legless Ghost Has Bosnians Spooked in Tuzla Bombsite: *Hartford* (Conn.) *Courant,* January 14, 1996; *Guardian,* January 30, 1996.

Spooked!: *Southampton Daily Echo,* October 28, 1995; *Scottish Daily Record,* February 3, 1996.

Images 105

Snapshot Picks up Ship's Crew's Prop-Chopped Chum: *Navy News,* May, 1996; *Daily Mail,* July 1, 1996.

Flying Manhole Cover: *Aberdeen Press and Journal,* September 9, 10, 1994; *Daily Record,* March 21, 1995; *Guardian,* March 25, 1995; *New Scientist,* April 8, 1995; *Ceefax,* November 21, 1995; *Daily Star,* July 7, 1993; *Sunday Mail* (Brisbane), August 27, 1995; *Guardian,* January 8, 1994.

Specter Shot in the Flames: *Daily Mail,* February 26, 1996; *Wolverhampton Express & Star,* February 26, 1996.

Bad Luck 108

Ballbuster: *Sunday Mirror,* September 3, 1995.

Around the World in a Daze: *Daily Telegraph,* February 5, 1996.

Win Some, Lose Some: *Lewiston Sun-Journal,* August 29, 1996; *Daily Telegraph,* August 30, 1996.

Falling Pray: *[AP],* July 16, 1996.

Out of the Frying Pan and into the Fire: *Guardian, Daily Mail, Western Morning News, Daily Telegraph,* August 11, 1994, August 8, 1995.

Fleshbombs!: *Toronto Globe and Mail,* December 14, 1994; *Daily Post,* August 20, 1994.

Good Luck 110

Cheesy Landing: *Sunday Express,* December 3, 1995.

First Alert: *Wolverhampton Express & Star,* November 3, 1995.

Golden Handshake: *Daily Record,* November 27, 1995.

Digital Discovery: *Scotsman,* May 25, 1996.

Saved by the Bell: *Daily Mail,* June 15, 1996.

Splat Marks the Spot: *San Francisco Chronicle,* July 7, 1996.

Sibling Serendipity: *Northern Echo,* February 23, 1996; *Guardian,* Sun, February 24, 1996; *Guardian,* January 27, 1996; *Sussex Evening Argus,* November 4, 1995; *Edinburgh Evening News,* February 2, 1996; *Daily Mirror,* December 30, 1995.

Second Wind: *Le Matin* (Lausanne, Switzerland), July 25, 1995.

Lucky for Some: *[AP],* July 24, 1996.

Blind Man at the Wheel: *[AP],* April 4, 1996.

Miracles 113

Milking It: unavailable.

Blinking Miracle: *Wolverhampton Express & Star,* May 17, 1995; *Southern Daily Echo,* August 17, 1995; *News of the World,* August 18, 1996.

(Un)Lucky: *[AP],* December 28, 1995.

Dames at Sea: *Daily Telegraph,* May 20, 1995; *Times,* September 9, 1995.

Holy Fruits: *Bolton Evening News,* March 12, 1996; *Manchester Evening News, Daily Mail,* March 13, 1996; *[AP], Asian Age,* February 27, 1996.

Nutter Sees Vision of Virgin: *[R],* July 8, 1996.

Monster Python's Healing Circus: *[AFP],* unnamed Indonesian paper, January 22, 1996.

Off the Wall: *[R],* December 28, 1995.

Poltergeists 116

Polts and Volts: *Edinburgh Evening News,* October 31, 1995.

In a Tizzy: *Yeovil Weekly News,* February 7, 1996; *Yeovil Express & Star,* March 14, 1996.

Hot Fashions: *South Wales Evening Post,* February 23, 1996; *Bristol Journal,* April 24, 1996; *Weekend Telegraph,* May 25, 1996.

"A/C, W/D, Lo Utils, Ghost": *Daily Mail,* October 29, 1993; The *European,* December 17–23, 1993.

Window Pains: *Sheffield Star,* February 13, 1996.

Eternal Flame: *Daily Telegraph,* December 17, 1995; *Yorkshire Evening Press,* January 5, 1996.

Strange Deaths: *Portsmouth News, Glasgow Herald, Guardian, Daily Mirror,* March 9, 1996; *Western Morning News,* March 21, 1996; *Wolverhampton Express & Star,* March 15, 1996; *Daily Express,* March 16, 1996; *[AP],* March 20, 1996; *Abend Zeitung,* April 6, 1995.

UFOs 119

Dunkin' UFOs: *Observer,* January 7, 1996.

British Airways Jet Buzzed by UFO: *Civil Aviation Authority Airmiss Report No. 2/95; Times,*February 2, 1996; *Daily Mail,* February 3, 1996; *Asian Age,* February 4, 1996.

China Saucer: *[AP],* December 31, 1995.

Alien Route: *Los Angeles Times,* February 3, 1996.

What Goes There?: *The Scotsman,* January 23, 1996.

Mystery Explosions: *[R],* January 26, 1996.

Asian UFO: *Victoria Times-Colonist,* October 25, 1995.

Haunted Housing: *Psychic News,* December 7, 1991; *Sun,* September 18, 1992; *Ceefax* (BBC1 Telextext), September 19, 1992; *Western Mail,* October 18, 1992, January 6, 1993.

Over the Moon about Alien Archaeology: *Enterprise Mission* news releases.

Feel a Presence: *Sun,* March 15, 1994;

News of the World, February 27, 1994; *Western Daily Press,* June 2, 1994; *The People,* June 5, 1994.

Close Encounters & Alien Abductions 124

Alien Presence at Bosnia Peace Talks: *Bufo's Weird World* (E-mail: bufo.cavin@awaiter.com), November 24, 1995.

Implants Out of This World: unavailable.

Implants Extracted: *Cleveland Plain Dealer,* November 8, 1995.

Isn't It Ironic?: *Expressen,* August 31, 1995; *Daily Record,* February 9, 1996; *Cumbrian Sunday News and Star,* September 3, 1995; *Weekly News,* March 23, 1996; *[R],* December 15, 1995.

Where's My Spaceship?: *[AFP],* January 27, 1996.

Galactic Snub for Bulgaria: *[AP],* September 12, 1995; *Romania Liberia,* September 15, 1995.

Brazil Nuts over Aliens: *AUFORA News Update,* May 30, June 2, and June 9, 1996; *International UFO Magazine,* July 1996; *ISCNIFlash,* July 16, 1996; *ISTO; Paranoia,* Spring 1996; *Wall Street Journal,* June 28, 1996.

Paranormal Experiences 129

Shattering Experience: *Expressen,* May 8, 1996.

Shocking Drip: *Sunday Express,* August 13, 1995.

Skinny: *Daily Mirror,* June 26, 1996.

Alarmingly Hot: *Aftenposten* (Norway), August 17, 1996.

Just a Coincidence . . . ?: *Sun,* June 2, 1995; *Sun,* October 31, 1995; *Building Magazine,* September 15, 1995; *Daily Mirror,* June 24, 1995; *Daily Telegraph,* February 21, 1996; *Edinburgh Evening News, Liverpool Echo,* June 6, 1995; *[AP],* January 5, 1996;

New York Post, January 6, 1996.

Mic Leads: *South China Morning Post,* July 29, 1996.

Elf Insurance: *[R],* October 18, 1995.

Tanks for Calling: *Washington Post,* October 17, 1995.

Look into My Eyes . . . : *Guardian,* August 27, 1996; *[R],* April 17, 1992.

Cornish Hum: *Cornishman,* November 2, 1995.

Dazed and Confused: *Daily Mirror,* August 3, 1996; *Evening Standard,* August 5, 1996.

PHOTO CREDITS

Cover
New Guinea Beans: Popperfoto/Reuter
Man with Lightbulb: Belfast Telegraph

The Human World
Kaneko/cross: AP
Tooth statue: Camerapress
Dirty Laundry: AP
Dead Wrong (Ashok): unavailable

The Animal World
Animal vs. Animal: Frank Spooner
Survivors: Bruce Coleman Collection
It's a New Mammal: Cincinnati Museum
   Center
Life, But Not: AP
Popobawa: Fortean Times
Chupacabras: unavailable
From Hull or Hell?: Ross Parry
Animal Anomalies: North News and
   Pictures

The Natural World
Crop Circles: Steve Alexander
Getting the Point: Rex Features
San Bernardo: Apex, AP TV
Livin' Large: *New York Daily News*
Tear: Sheffield Star
On the Rocks: Dr. Peter Wadhams

The Paranormal World
Cyberspoons: All Action
Milk/Ganesh: Popperfoto/Reuters
Navy Chop: Mrs. Bobbie Capel
Flamed: Caters
Brazil Alien: unavailable
Over the Moon: NASA
UFO of British Airways: Fortean
   Times

WELCOME TO THE WORLD OF THE BIZARRE AND THE BEWILDERING

From UFOs, Bigfoot and visions of the Virgin Mary to weird tales and human oddities, *Fortean Times* is a respected chronicler of strange phenomena with 24 years' experience of reporting from wild frontiers. Informed, open-minded, skeptical, and above all extremely funny, FT has the lowdown on what's out there.

Write or call for details of our latest subscription offers. Or send for a sample issue for just $4.95. (You can pay by credit card using our order hotline, or with a check payable to Fenner, Reed & Jackson.)

"The only thing predictable about *Fortean Times* is that it will be unpredictable, which makes it great fun to read."
—*The Boston Globe*

"Immensely entertaining. . . . A great, roaring sense of humor."
—*Contra Costa Times*

"Bringing wit and erudition to outlandish subject matter."
—*The New York Times*

"Possibly the most entertaining publication on the planet."
—*Wired*

FORTEAN TIMES,
Box 754
Manhasset, NY 11030-0754
Phone (516) 627 3836.
Fax (516) 627 1972.
Or e-mail
sgrudnick@aol.com

THE TRUTH IS IN HERE!

ISBN: 0-8362-1499-4

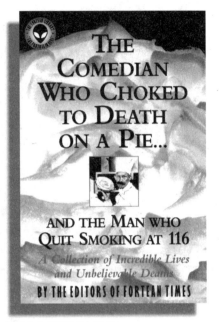

ISBN: 0-8362-2147-8

Plumb the mysteries of the megabeaver, follow worldwide cataclysms from fiery floods to giant sinkholes, meet the Enema Bandit, and mourn the South American chef who was stabbed through the heart with uncooked spaghetti strands when his restaurant was hit by 150 mph winds. A real-life *X-Files* with a sense of humor, *Strange Days #1* is a dizzying romp through the most extraordinary events of our day, from UFOs and poltergeists to natural wonders, zany coincidences, and just plain head-scratching incidents.

People do the funniest things, in life and in death, and this compendium from the editors of *Fortean Times* brings together true tales of the hilarious deaths and bizarrely triumphant lives of ordinary folks from around the world. *The Comedian Who Choked to Death on a Pie . . . and the Man who Quit Smoking at 116* gathers together hundreds of comic demises with a cast of over 50 centenarians, revealing fascinating and funny insights into how to live, and how not to.